Queen Mary *departs from New York on another dash across the Atlantic* (Frank O. Braynard Collection).

FLAGSHIPS OF THE LINE

FLAGSHIPS OF THE LINE

A celebration of the world's three-funnel liners

Milton H. Watson

Patrick Stephens

Dedication

To
Frank O. Braynard
An inspiration and a dedicated
maritime scholar

First published in 1988

British Library Cataloguing in Publication Data

Watson, Milton H
Flagships of the line : a celebration of
the world's three-funnel liners.
1. Ocean liners—History
I. Title
387.2'432   VM381

ISBN   0-85059-931-8

*Patrick Stephens Limited is part of the
Thorsons Publishing Group,
Wellingborough, Northamptonshire,
NN 8 2RQ, England*

Printed in Great Britain by The Bath Press, Bath,
Avon

1   3   5   7   9   10   8   6   4   2

Contents

Acknowledgements

Within the last five years there have been several books written on passenger liners, individual companies and even the four-stack ocean greyhounds, but nothing was dedicated to three-funnel steamers. Therefore I decided that this volume would be a fitting tribute to 56 of the finest ocean liners ever commissioned.

No work of this calibre could be undertaken without the active support of knowledgeable experts, and to one, Frank O. Braynard, maritime historian *extraordinaire,* I am indebted. At his home in Sea Cliff, Long Island, he led me down a flight of stairs into a labyrinth of filing cabinets beaming with brochures and photographs. He allowed me to select the most ravishing pictures, then supplied tit-bits of information about the ships. Also, my thanks to Richard Morse who provided a selection of choice pictures from his valuable collection. Finally, I thank Laura Brown, librarian of the Steamship Historical Society of America Collection at the University of Baltimore (whose pic-tures are credited here 'SSHA Collection') who assisted me in locating brochures and photographs during and after my many visits to the library.

Additional persons and companies who lent a helping hand with information and/or photographs were: Dave Jones, Canadian Pacific Corporate Archives; Compagnie Générale Maritime; Mr R. Alexander, Furness Withy Group; Hamburg-South America Line; Roy Feuck, Hapag-Lloyd AG; The Illustrated London News Picture Library; The Mariners' Museum, Newport News, Virginia; Stephen Rabson, P & O; Peabody Museum, Salem, Mass; South Street Seaport Museum, New York; United States National Archives, Washington, DC; and World Ship Society Photo Library.

To Terry Fenster, who took time away from her busy schedule to proof-read my manuscript, should go a round of thanks, and a very special thanks to Patrick Stephens Limited for accepting this work.

Foreword
by William H. Miller

The first ship, passenger or otherwise, that I ever stepped aboard was a three-stacker. The date was May 1953 and the vessel the beloved *Queen of Bermuda*. My grandparents were sailing, bound for a vacation to that ideal vacation spot some 600 miles south of New York City.

If the single-stackers were mostly sleek and raked, and the twin-stackers possibly the very best examples of shipping design, proportion and balance, the three-stackers were, for the most part, majestic and stately. I can recall seeing so clearly in the confines of New York harbour two of the best-looking triple-funnel liners: the aforementioned Furness ship and Cunard's exceptional *Queen Mary*. Indeed, their three funnels—akin to three crowns—gave them majesty. More specifically, I have indelible memories of their steam whistles, especially when they sounded these simultaneously from the first and second stacks.

In his second book, Milton Watson provides us with a parade of three-stackers. The likes of the *Queen Mary,* the extraordinary *Normandie* and the innovative *Ile de France* are perhaps the most widely known, best remembered and universally appreciated. Almost equally as large and important were Albert Ballin's brilliant pre-First World War trio of *Imperator, Vaterland* and *Bis-marck*, which might be best remembered in their subsequent 'second lives' as the *Berengaria, Leviathan* and *Majestic* respectively. There are others of special note as well—the superb transatlantic *Paris*, another Frenchman, the ill-fated *L'Atlantique*, some Canadian Pacific 'Empresses' including *Empress of Britain*, their North Atlantic flagship, and *Empress of Japan,* their premier ship in transpacific operation, and P&O's first 'Strath' liners, the *Strathaird* and *Strathnaver*.

But there are also a good number of smaller, lesser-known, perhaps mostly forgotten, three-stackers. These include the likes of British India's *Tairea,* Canadian National's *Prince Henry* and the French *Mariette Pacha*. These were important, and very charming ships as well. They spark my mind to reflect, at least momentarily, of some colourful poster, say from the evocative 1930s, depicting a moonlit exotic port. It might have been the *Naldera* at Suez, the *Cap Polonio* at Rio or the *Patria* at Dakar.

Indeed, the three-stackers, a special group of ocean liners, were *Flagships of the Line*.

Bill Miller
Jersey City, New Jersey

Introduction

Seeking ways to lure passengers to their liners, steamship executives were constantly on the prowl for new and innovative ideas. The concept of placing three funnels on an ocean liner began a new era.

The primary purpose of the funnel was to emit burnt fuel, exhaust fumes and smut clear of the decks and upward into the sky, while the outer surface was used to carry the owner's colours. *City of Rome,* the first three-funnel liner, launched the imperial age of shipping in 1881. The funnels became the icon of power, luxury and prestige. In 1888, safety was added to these attributes; emigrants were known to ask how many stacks their steamer had, for they were reluctant to travel in a vessel with one or two. Therefore, with such profits to be realized from increased and hopefully loyal patronage, it was not surprising that shipping executives rushed to order three-funnel liners. In all, a total of 56 such ships were constructed, of which 38 were flagships of the fleet at the time of their commissioning. Sybaritic liners at the time of their completion, they sailed the oceans proudly displaying the flag of their nation and the funnel colours of their owners.

Many of the three-stackers had illustrious careers, like *Ile de France* and *Queen Mary*. Others changed hands frequently as *Resolute* and *Reliance* did, and a few, such as *Cap Trafalgar* and *L'Atlantique*, met premature ends. The stories of all are told here in alphabetical order according to the owning company, with each of their liners listed chronologically.

To enhance the work I have included fares, based on double occupancy per person for summer season travel. They are given in both sterling and dollars, the equivalents being based on contemporary exchange rates. Though the fares may seem low by today's standards, it must be remembered that wages were also low. In 1935, for example, a British male manual worker earned only an average of £3 5s ($15.70) a week; two decades later, the figure had gone up to only £11 3s ($31.40). In the first half of the century especially, families were large and times were hard for the average person, both in Europe and the USA, and a comfortable middle class with a discretionary income did not exist until after 1945. Therefore the bulk of the first and second class passengers until the 1950s were the well-to-do—the Rockefellers, DuPonts, Morgans and royalty—film stars, literary personalities and merchants. Third class and steerage passengers were usually emigrants, and, in the case of the North Atlantic after the 1920s, eastbound and westbound customers were professors, college students, struggling artists, shop-owners, etc.

Literature on some of the ships and companies is voluminous, while for lesser-known liners and firms, information had to be gathered piecemeal, and, where available, company literature of the period was examined. The statistics for each ship were obtained from *Lloyds Registry of Shipping* although in some issues of *Lloyds* the length was listed between perpendiculars, whereas other works listed length overall. Therefore, to be consistent with other maritime specialists, the latter length measurement has been adopted except in the case of those ships whose length is marked 'bp' where the former measurement applies.

The last three-stacker was withdrawn from service in 1967. She was the legendary *Queen Mary*, and today she is embedded in cement at Long Beach, California, and serves as a hotel, convention centre and maritime museum. Meanwhile, Windstar Cruises has built two ships powered by both diesel-electric engines and sails. Could it be in the not too distant future that a three-funnel liner is built for nostalgia's sake?

Milton H. Watson
Bronx, New York

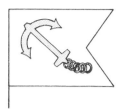

Anchor Line

Columbia

(Moreas)

Builders D. & W. Henderson Ltd, Glasgow, 1902
Specifications 8,292 tons; 486 ft (148 m) long (bp), 56 ft (17 m) wide
Machinery Triple expansion engines; twin screw; speed 16 knots
Passengers 345 first class, 218 second class, 740 third class
Demise Scrapped in 1929

By the late 1890s, Anchor Line had begun contemplating a replacement for their ageing dowager *City of Rome* of 1882 fame. An order was placed with D. & W. Henderson, and the product that emerged in 1902 was the bilge keel, three-funnel liner *Columbia*. After successful sea trials, *Columbia*, Anchor Line's new flagship, commenced her maiden voyage from Glasgow on 17 May 1902. After a brief call at Moville, in Donegal, Ireland, she proceeded to New York.

Anchor Line's first three-funnel liner, Columbia *(R. Loren Graham, SSHSA Collection).*

Columbia was an instant success and she became a regular visitor on her voyages up and down the Clyde every fourth weekend, her three pipe-stem funnels identifying her to the least experienced maritime watcher on the shore. To capitalize on *Columbia's* good fortunes, Anchor placed an order for a larger ship that appeared in 1905 as the two-funnel *Caledonia*.

Passenger accommodation was distributed through six decks. First class cabins were situated amidships with berths for one, two or three passengers. There was a 'capacious and handsome' main saloon, a library with a fine selection of books, drawing-rooms and music-rooms and 'illuminated decks with their magnificent promenades—indeed, all accommodations are such as to appeal to people of refinement'. Second class rooms were 'commodious and comfortable' and the second class passengers enjoyed the use of a dining-room with their own stewards, a music-room and smoking-room and spacious decks. In fact, they were provided with all the necessaries for the voyage, including a liberal and varied bill of fare. Cabins were for two, three and four persons.

Columbia remained on the North Atlantic until she was requisitioned by the Royal Navy as the armed merchant cruiser *Columbella* in November 1914. After five years in grey, she was returned to Anchor in 1919.

Anchor reverted her name to *Columbia*, and as such she resumed sailing in August 1919 with a capacity for 72 first, 430 second and 378 third class passengers. Two years later she was converted to burn fuel oil. Changing times and clientele altered *Columbia's* capacity in November 1922 to 492 cabin and 420 third. Growing old in the face of newer tonnage, she made her last Anchor sailing from Glasgow in August 1925. In all, *Columbia* completed 208 round voyages and carried a total of 165,789 passengers. Upon returning to Glasgow, she was laid up in the River Clyde until purchased in 1926 by the British firm Byron Steamship Company Ltd.

Byron renamed its acquisition *Moreas*, revised her capacity to the original figures then dispatched her from Piraeus on 1 September 1926 for New York. She made three round trips for the company before being laid up in 1927. The next

year saw *Moreas* transferred to the National Greek Line, but she never sailed for them. Instead, she remained laid up until July 1929 when she sailed to Venice to be scrapped.

Transylvania

Builders Fairfield Shipbuilding & Engineering Co Ltd, Glasgow, 1925
Specifications 16,923 gross tons; 552 ft (168 m) long, 70 ft (21 m) wide
Machinery Steam turbines; twin screw; speed 16 knots
Passengers 279 first class, 344 second class, 800 third class
Demise Torpedoed in 1940

Laid down in December 1919, *Transylvania* was not launched until March 1925, and completed six months later. Unlike her near sisters, the *Tuscania* and *California* with one funnel, *Transylvania* and her sister *Caledonia* were given three funnels for streamlining effect—the first and third funnels were dummies.

Transylvania was placed on the Glasgow-Moville-New York run, which she first made on 12 September 1925 from Glasgow. She quickly settled in and, together with the other three ships, Anchor Line offered a commendable first class service between Scotland and the United States.

First class public rooms were concentrated on the Promenade Deck and included a lounge, garden lounge, writing-room, corridor lounge, smoking-room and verandah cafe. An elevator connected the various accommodation decks and the dining-room down below. Second class (tourist after 1930) was described as 'luxury without ostentation'; there were home-like social halls (smoking-room and lounge with upright piano and plants), gleaming dining-room and spacious promenades and play decks. The brochure assured passengers that 'there is a generous roominess which insures complete freedom from congestion and discomfort'.

During *Transylvania's* career, she was involved in one near rescue mission and a collision. Three days out from Glasgow on 22 November 1928,

Transylvania all dressed up (R. Loren Graham, SSHSA Collection).

she responded to an SOS from the German steamer *Herrenwyk*. However, rough seas prevented *Transylvania* from lowering her lifeboats and another respondent, the Baltic-American liner *Estonia*, also stood by but was hampered by heavy seas. After standing by for 15 hours, *Transylvania* proceeded to New York, whereas *Estonia* managed to lower a lifeboat and rescued the German crew. Within four months, *Transylvania* was again in the news. Nearing the end of a Mediterranean cruise that commenced in January at New York, *Transylvania* ran aground. It occurred at about 5 am in dense fog on 28 March 1929 on La Cocque, a dangerous rock near the Jardeheu Semaphore, ten miles west of Cherbourg. Many passengers were up and about and the impact caused a grinding crash and list that frightened some of them into confusion. The crew quickly assembled them and calm was restored shortly afterwards, whereupon they were taken ashore. The passengers' luggage, along with items in the cargo, was removed to lighten the ship, enabling her to float off the

rocks around 6 pm. *Transylvania* then proceeded to Cherbourg for hull inspection before sailing for Glasgow for repairs that lasted until June of that year.

Changing with the times, Anchor remodelled *Transylvania's* classes to first, tourist and third in October 1930, and again in March 1936 to cabin, tourist and third. During the winter months, *Transylvania* was sent cruising from New York; the Caribbean was the most frequent destination. Others included an 88-day voyage entitled 'The Great African Cruise' that departed from New York on 17 January 1931, and to enjoy which passengers paid a minimum of $1,450 (£299). The year after the last of the superliners arrived on the scene in 1936, Anchor decided to ensure its share of the trans-Atlantic market by extensively reconditioning *Transylvania*.

She made her final departure from New York as a passenger liner on 30 August 1939, and upon arrival in England was taken over by the Admiralty and converted into an armed merchant cruiser. In that role, *Transylvania* was torpedoed and sunk by German submarine U56 on 10 August 1940, 35 miles west of Inishtrahull, Northern Ireland. Forty-eight people perished.

Caledonia *in New York* (R. Loren Graham, SSHSA Collection).

Caledonia

(Scotstoun)

Builders A. Stephen & Sons, Glasgow, 1925
Specifications 17,046 tons; 552 ft (168 m) long, 70 ft (21 m) wide
Machinery Steam turbines; twin screw; speed 16 knots
Passengers 205 first class, 403 second class, 796 third class
Demise Torpedoed in 1940

The keel of *Caledonia* was laid down in February 1920, but due to the changing US immigration laws, Anchor Line was hesitant about completing the ship. The executives decided, however, that an extra hull could do no harm and decided to continue her building. Launched in 1925, *Caledonia* was completed in October. With smoke billowing from her second funnel (the first and third were dummies). Anchor's new flagship, departed from Glasgow for Moville (Ireland) and New York on 3 October 1925.

In 1930, 1936 and 1938 Caledonia's accommodation was remodelled to placate the new traveller, the American heading east on vacation. For those lucky few with time and money to travel, the minimum rate for an eight-day voyage from New York to Glasgow in 1935 was $155 (£32) first class, $112.50 (£23.30) tourist class and $80.50 (£16.67) third class.

During the late 1920s and early 1930s, *Caledonia*, along with many veteran trans-Atlantic steamers, could be found cruising the warmer climates during the off season. Among her more notable ventures was a 125-day round-the-world cruise that departed from New York on 16 January 1928 with rates from $1,250 to $3,800 (£257.73 to £783.50) and a series of nine-day 'Millionaire Cruises' in 1933 to the Caribbean at tariffs from $98.50 (£24.50) for an inside cabin with two lower berths to $575 (£143) for a Parlour Suite.

Caledonia undertook her last commercial sailing from New York on 27 June 1939. Three months later, the Admiralty acquired her and named her *Scotstoun*. She carried troops and supplies as an armed merchant cruiser until she was torpedoed by German submarine U25 on 13 June 1940, 80 miles west of Barra Island, Hebrides. Six people lost their lives.

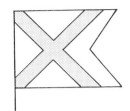

British India Steam Navigation Company

Tairea

Builders Barclay, Curle & Company, Glasgow, 1924
Specifications 7,933 gross tons; 465 ft (141 m) long, 60 ft (18 m) wide
Machinery Triple expansion; twin screw; speed 16 knots
Passengers 56 first class, 80 second class
Demise Scrapped 1952.

Tairea *sailed in Asian and African waters* (P & O Group).

Tairea was the first of three sister ships built for British India's Calcutta/Far East service. Each of the trio was built with three stacks (the third one was a dummy) to supposedly impress the Chinese customers as to their speed, safety and power.

Tairea was handed over to BI in May 1924, and commenced sailing from Calcutta to Kobe calling at Penang, Singapore, Hong Kong, Amoy, Shanghai, Moji and Yokohama. In 1932 she was transferred to the Bombay/East Africa/Durban service.

In 1939, *Tairea* was converted into the hospi-

tal ship HT35 and served in the Somaliland campaign, moving between Kismayu and Mogadishu and taking off wounded from the beach-heads. After involvement in the Madagascar operations of 1942, she moved to the Mediterranean where she spent the rest of the war.

British India returned *Tairea* to the Calcutta/Far East run after the war and she survived on the route until sold on 1 April 1952 to the British Iron & Steel Corporation to be scrapped at Blyth.

Takliwa

Builders Barclay, Curle & Company, Glasgow, 1924
Specifications 7,936 gross tons; 465 ft (141 m) long, 60 ft (18 m) wide
Machinery Triple expansion engines; twin screw; speed 16 knots
Passengers 56 first class, 80 second class
Demise Burned in 1945

The second of British India's three-funnel trio to enter service was *Takliwa*, which commenced operation in July 1924. She too served on the India/Straits/China and Japan services, and between 1933 and 1939 operated the Bombay/East Africa/Durban service. Ports of call southbound were Porebunder, Marmagoa, Seychelles, Mombasa, Zanzibar, Dar-es-Salaam, Mozambique and Lourenço Marques (Maputo). The voyage took approximately 21 days and first class fares between Bombay and Durban in 1937 were £48 ($235), and £33 ($164) in second class.

Takliwa was taken over by the Navy and used as a troop-ship during the war, being present at the landings at Syracuse and Augusta in Sicily. On 15 October 1945 she was stranded and burned out in the South Nicobar Islands; it can be presumed that she burned as a troop-ship since the war had ended only two months before.

Takliwa *spent her career out of Calcutta and Bombay (P & O Group).*

Above *A close-up of British India's* Talamba *(P & O Group).*

Below Talamba *aground at Lyemun Point on 2 September 1937 (P & O Group).*

Talamba

Builders Hawthorn, Leslie & Company, Newcastle, 1924
Specifications 8,018 gross tons; 466 ft (142 m) long, 60 ft (18 m) wide
Machinery Triple expansion engines; twin screw; speed 16 knots
Passengers 56 first class, 60 second class, 4,108 deck
Demise Bombed in 1943

The last of the BI trio was *Talamba*, delivered on 1 October 1924. Like her two sisters, she was placed on the Calcutta–Kobe run, by way of Penanga, Singapore, Hong Kong, Amoy, Shanghai, Moji and Yokohama, where she spent her entire career. Unlike *Tairea* and *Takliwa*, however, *Talamba* was fitted to carry over 4,000 people on deck. This number was later reduced to 2,777.

During a typhoon on 2 September 1937, *Talamba* was blown ashore at Lyemun Point, Hong Kong. She was refloated on 21 November 1937 and after undergoing repairs was placed back in service.

At the outbreak of hostilities, she was taken over and converted into a troop-ship, then in 1940 she was converted to a hospital ship. *Talamba* served in Eastern waters and in the Mediterranean, including being present at the Sicily landings in 1943.

On the night of 10 July 1943, the fully-illuminated *Talamba* was embarking wounded three miles off the Avola Anchorage, Sicily, when at around 10 pm she was bombed by German aircraft. She started to sink and the 400 wounded were taken off by other ships. Only five of *Talamba*'s crew of 168 were killed.

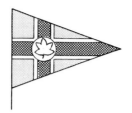

Canadian National Railways

Prince Robert
(Charlton Sovereign, Lucania)

Builders Cammell, Laird & Company Ltd, Birkenhead, 1930
Specifications 6,893 gross tons; 366 ft (111 m) long, 57 ft (17 m) wide
Machinery Steam turbines; twin screw; speed 23 knots
Passengers 319 first class, 46 deck
Demise Scrapped in 1962

In the 1920s, Canadian National Railways decided to break the Canadian Pacific's monopoly on the intracoastal trade in the Pacific north-west by ordering three identical ships that would challenge CP's 'Princesses' on the tri-city service between Vancouver, Victoria and Seattle. The first to arrive at Vancouver from England was *Prince Robert* in 1930, followed that year in quick succession by *Prince Henry* and *Prince David*. All were dispatched on the Vancouver-Victoria-Seattle service with a call at Prince Rupert, CN's rail terminus.

Passengers had the use of five decks. The lowest was C-Deck where the dining-room was located aft, and above on B-Deck were mainly cabins, with a small Georgian Court aft. Next up was A-Deck containing cabins and a music salon aft; this was followed by Promenade Deck where an observation lounge was forward, followed by two-berth cabins with an Old English smoking-room aft. Sun Deck was available for deck sports and tanning. All cabins were outside, with 42 cabins possessing private facilities. Decor and furnishings were modest and in tune with the ships' route.

The Depression affected all businesses, and the CN tri-city service suffered accordingly. Canadian Pacific proved themselves the better company, and, with revenue down, CN withdrew from the service in September, 1931. *Prince Robert* sailed east to undertake three trips between Boston and the West Indies, one trip from Halifax to South America and one trip between Halifax and Vancouver. From 13 June to 31 August 1932, she was employed on the Vancouver-Alaska service calling at Prince Rupert, Ketchikan, Taku, Glacier Bay and Juneau, completing the round trip in seven days, with the minimum fare starting at $90 (£24.50) for an outside upper and lower. Following a two-year lay-up, she commenced summer sailings in 1935 which were advertised as cruises, and she undertook four such voyages that year. Each lasted 11 days, offering many ports of call for $100 (£20.70) to $215 (£44.51) for a de luxe suite with sitting-room, two lower beds and a private bath. These cruises were repeated each year until 1939.

When Britain declared war on Germany in 1939, all British ships were requisitioned by the Admiralty. *Prince Robert* was called to duty that year and was extensively rebuilt into an anti-aircraft cruiser with two funnels. She served world-wide, calling at ports in the Pacific, Indian and Mediterranean regions. Decommissioned in 1948, she was purchased by Charlton Steam

Prince Robert, *built for the tri-city service* (W. B. Taylor, SSHSA Collection).

Shipping Company, a Greek shipping firm headed by one Mr Chandris. Taken into a shipyard, the ship, now a little shabby, was refitted to carry refugees. Given the name *Charlton Sovereign* and listed at 5,516 gross tons, she operated between Europe, South America and Australia until 1951 when engine trouble forced Charlton to offer her for sale.

What seemed an unlikely candidate for further sailing was purchased by the Italian firm of Fratelli Grimaldi. Sent to an Italian yard, the ship was extensively rebuilt as their *Lucania*. Her straight stem was lengthened by fifteen feet and given a sharp rake, modern funnels replaced the utilitarian exhausts and her superstructure was built up forward to accommodate first class public rooms. Boasting two outdoor swimming-pools and accommodation for over 700 passengers in two classes, *Lucania*, now 6,723 gross tons, commenced sailings in 1952 on Grimaldi's

Italy–West Indies run. When, however, she became outclassed by larger tonnage, she was laid up in 1962, becoming the last ship to wear Grimaldi colours. She was subsequently broken up that year at Vado, near Leghorn.

Prince Henry
(North Star, Empire Parkeston)

Builders Cammell, Laird & Company Ltd, Birkenhead, 1930
Specifications 6,893 gross tons; 366 ft (111 m) long, 57 ft (17 m) wide
Machinery Steam turbines; twin screw; speed 23 knots
Passengers 331 first class, 46 deck
Demise Scrapped in 1952

Prince Henry was the second vessel to join the CN tri-city fleet in 1930. Together with her sisters, *Prince Robert* and the forthcoming *Prince David*, she provided frequent services between Vancouver, Victoria and Seattle. In the summer of 1931, the *Prince Henry* was taken off the tri-city service and placed on the Vancouver-Skagway run, completing the round trip in seven days. After the summer season, CN incurred heavy deficits and they decided to withdraw from the tri-city service. Consequently, *Prince Henry* was laid up in September 1931.

In 1932, *Prince Henry* was transferred to the East Coast and made 24 round trips between Boston and Bermuda and three trips between Boston and Havana. She was then laid up at Halifax, and did not return to service until 1936 when she made five West Indies cruises from Halifax under the operation of National Tours. During the spring of 1937, she operated six cruises from Miami to Vera Cruz, then later that year was chartered to the Canadian firm of Clarke Steamship Company, who eventually purchased her in December 1938. After a modest refit at a local shipyard, the vessel was renamed

Prince Henry *spent her early years laid up* (W. B. Taylor, SSHSA Collection).

North Star and utilized as a 'cruise ship'.

All cabins were outside, with the majority on B-Deck possessing private facilities. Her public rooms were scattered over four decks—C-Deck was the lowest and located aft, only feet away from the propellers, was the dining-room featuring French cuisine. Above it on B-Deck was the Georgian Court. Aft on A Deck was the music salon with grand piano, and on Promenade Deck (forward) was the observation lounge and (aft) the Old English smoking-room. In between were forty two-berth cabins without private bathrooms.

North Star's typical schedule would be winters and springs out of Miami and summers and autumns sailing from New York; most of her cruises were seven days in length. The *North Star*'s winter 1939 programme called for seven-day cruises from Miami to Port-au-Prince, Kingston and Havana. An outside cabin with upper and lower berths without private facilities cost $75 (£16) and a de luxe suite with two lower beds, sitting-room and private facilities was $220 (£45). During the summer months she sailed one

B 156 885 1930

way between New York and Montreal, calling at Nova Scotia, Newfoundland, Labrador and Quebec on a cruise lasting 11½ days. The 1939 tariffs ranged from $145 (£31) for an upper and lower berth cabin to $375 (£81) for a suite consisting of twin bedrooms, sitting-room, luggage room, tub bath and toilet. The return occupied a further 11 days and the rates were $10 (£2) to $25 (£5) less. For passengers lacking the time to cruise back to New York, Clarke Steamship Company provided them with the option of returning by plane at $18 (£4), train at $12 (£3), or bus for $8 (£2).

At the outbreak of war, *North Star* was requisitioned by the British Admiralty. Overhaul for military duty included the removal of one funnel, following which she participated in the invasion of Normandy and served the allies admirably. Following hostilities, she was briefly laid up and eventually purchased in 1946 by the Ministry of War Transport. They converted her, and in March 1947 she emerged as the 5,556 tons *Empire Parkeston,* with austere accommodation for 813 troops. She was placed under the management of General Steam Navigation Company and became a British Army of Occupation, Rhine (BAOR) leave ship. From 1948, *Empire Parkeston* was regularly employed as a troop ferry between Harwich and the Hook of Holland, and usually covered the 116-mile voyage in seven to

eight hours travelling at 16 knots. Her only deviation from the route was in 1956 when she sailed to the Mediterranean during the Suez crisis and to Cardiff the following year to transport the Welsh Guards to Holland.

In 1961, defence cutbacks necessitated her retirement. She was laid up in September and subsequently sold and towed to La Spezia in February 1962 for scrapping by Lotti SpA.

Prince David

(Marlton Monarch)

Builders Cammell, Laird & Company Ltd, Birkenhead, 1930
Specifications 6,892 gross tons; 366 ft (111 m) long, 57 ft (17 m) wide
Machinery Steam turbines; twin screw; speed 23 knots
Passengers 331 first class, 46 deck
Demise Scrapped in 1951

The last of the trio ordered by CN in the 1920s was *Prince David.* She was placed like her sisters on the tri-city service between Vancouver, Victoria and Seattle with a call at Prince Rupert. The service was not a success and in the autumn of 1932 *Prince David* was transferred to the Atlantic coast where she made cruises from Boston, New

Above left *The cruise ship* North Star (Malley, SSHSA Collection).

Above Prince David *in white livery for cruises* (Everett E. Viez, SSHSA Collection).

Right *The Observation Rooom of* Prince David (Everett E. Viez, SSHSA Collection).

Right *The cosy Smoking Room on board* Prince David (Everett E. Viez, SSHSA Collection).

York and Miami under the Canadian National banner.

On one such cruise in 1932 misfortune struck. En route from Boston to Bermuda on 13 March, *Prince David* struck a reef near Hamilton and nearly sank. Headlines in one paper read '80 saved as Bermuda steamer sinks' and an illustration showed the crippled ship sinking stern first. Fortunately, she was pumped out, towed to Boston and repaired. Her place for the remainder of 1932 was taken by *Prince Henry*. *Prince David*

was returned to service in 1934 for 43 trips between Miami and Nassau and between 1936 and 1937 for cruises out of New York, after which she was laid up at Halifax until requisitioned for war duty in 1939.

Prince David was requisitioned for war duty in 1939. After strenuous service, she was released in 1948 and immediately purchased by Charlton Steam Shipping Company. Renamed *Charlton Monarch,* she was refitted, like her sister *Charlton Sovereign,* to carry refugees from Europe to South America and Australia, before age and engine trouble necessitated her sale in 1951 to the scrapyard.

Prince David, *one-quarter submerged* (Frank O. Braynard Collection).

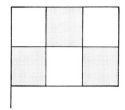

Canadian Pacific

Empress of Russia

Builders Fairfield Shipbuilding & Engineering
Co Ltd, Glasgow, 1913
Specifications 16,810 gross tons; 592 ft (180 m)
long, 68 ft (21 m) wide
Machinery Steam turbines; quadruple screw;
speed 20 knots
Passengers 284 first class, 100 second class, 808
Asiatic steerage
Demise Scrapped in 1946

Canadian Pacific was incorporated on 16 February 1881 to build a railroad across Canada, linking the Atlantic with the Pacific. Once the line was completed, the company needed ships to carry the freight and passengers across the Pacific; it therefore entered the shipping business in 1884, confining its activities to the Lake Superior and Lake Huron areas before branching out across the Pacific in 1891. In 1911, Canadian Pacific ordered a pair of liners to supplement their Pacific duo of *Empress of India* and *Empress of Japan*. At the cost of $5 million for the pair, the first to make her appearance was *Empress of Russia*, launched on 28 August 1912 by Mrs W. Beauclerk, daughter of CP's president Sir Thomas Shaughnessy, and completed on 22 March 1913. Her distinction as CP's flagship lasted only three months. The white hulled *Empress of Russia* departed from Liverpool on 1 April 1913 with a party of round-the-world passengers and proceeded to Yokohama via the Mediterranean,

Suez Canal, Colombo, Singapore, Hong Kong, Shanghai and Nagasaki. On leaving Yokohama, she headed for Vancouver, arriving on 29 May 1914 after 9 days 5 hours 29 minutes at an average speed of 19.86 knots, a record she held for nine years. *Empress of Russia*, along with her sister ship *Empress of Asia*, spent the next few months zipping across the Pacific as the first large liners to have cruiser sterns. Because of their speed, the Philippine government requested that Manila be a port of call and the request was fulfilled on 29 June 1914 when *Empress of Russia* called there for the first time.

On 22 August 1914, *Empress of Russia* was requisitioned by the Royal Navy at Hong Kong and utilized as an armed merchant cruiser, serving mainly in the Indian Ocean. On 2 December 1916, she was returned to Canadian Pacific by the Royal Navy who felt that she and the other large liners had been improperly utilized for the war effort. Canadian Pacific placed the 'Empress' back on the transpacific run, but when the war reached a turning point and the need for further transports arose, *Empress of Russia* was requisitioned again in 1918 and sailed as a troop transport ferrying soldiers across the Atlantic.

Hostilities over, *Empress of Russia* was given an overhaul in Hong Kong and resumed service in 1919 with a capacity for 350 first class, 70 second class, 90 third class and 728 steerage class passengers. She settled down with her consorts plying the Pacific from Vancouver to Yokohama, Shanghai, Hong Kong and Manila, completing six round trips annually. Honolulu was added

Above *The Pacific 'speed queen' for nine years,* Empress of Russia (Canadian Pacific).

Below *The camouflage-painted* Empress of Russia *during the First World War* (Richard Morse Collection).

The first class lounge in Empress of Russia (Canadian Pacific).

in the early 1930s. Passage fares in dollars (pounds) for 1933 were as follows:

Vancouver to:	First	Tourist	Third	Servants	
				European	Oriental
Honolulu	110 (27)	70 (17)	55 (14)	110 (27)	50 (12)
Yokohama	285 (71)	160 (40)	60 (15)	228 (57)	55 (14)
Shanghai	331 (83)	185 (46)	85 (21)	265 (66)	80 (20)
Hong Kong	360 (90)	200 (50)	87.50 (22)	288 (72)	82.50 (21)
Manila	360 (90)	200 (50)	95 (24)	288 (72)	90 (23)

Though the rates seem reasonable by today's standards, the Far East was basically a region for colonial civil servants and merchants with business to conduct. Tourism was restricted to the annual visits of world cruise liners. Also, the fares give an indication of the racial hierarchy of the period. European servants travelled at slightly lower rates than first class passengers and took their meals in a dining-room, while the Asian servants were charged less than third class rates and were kept apart from their European colleagues.

Empress of Russia arrived in Vancouver after the Second World War was declared. She was defensively armed with anti-submarine and anti-aircraft guns, painted grey and then dispatched across the Pacific on her regular schedule under naval instructions. After completing 310 trans-pacific crossings, she was called upon again to serve her country. In November 1940 she was requisitioned at Hong Kong and proceeded to Vancouver, calling at Australia, New Zealand, Suva, Fiji and Honolulu, then sailed through the Panama Canal to the Clyde where she was fitted as a troop transport. In April 1941 she was sent to South Africa, Suez, South Africa, Puerto Rico, Newport News, Halifax and, finally, the Clyde. At San Juan, Puerto Rico, the Chinese crew, who were not allowed ashore in many countries, were finally able to stretch their legs. In fact a

The remains of Empress of Russia *after the fire* (Richard Morse Collection).

few did not return, leaving the ship short of firemen. In 1942 she made a number of trips to South Africa, one of which was extended to Bombay and Colombo.

After participating in the North African landings in July 1943, *Empress of Russia* was transferred to special duties. She was the only large coal-burning transport left, and she presented problems in the lack of good steam coal and good firemen. She was now confined to 'local' waters, making a prisoner exchange trip to Gothenburg in October 1943 followed by seven trips to Reykjavik, Iceland. In October 1944, *Empress of Russia* was laid up at Gareloch. She had steamed 160,056 miles under five masters and carried 53,850 military personnel, 5,486 prisoners of war, 904 civilians and 6,230 tons of cargo.

During the spring of 1945, naval command thought she would make a good ship in which to repatriate Canadian troops. To get her in shape for her new role, she was taken to Barrow for a refit during which, on 8 September 1945, *Empress of Russia* was totally destroyed by fire. She was sold to T. W. Ward & Sons and broken up at Barrow in 1946.

Empress of Asia

Builders Fairfield Shipbuilding & Engineering Co Ltd, Glasgow, 1913
Specifications 16,909 gross tons; 592 ft (180 m) long, 68 ft (21 m) wide
Machinery Steam turbines; quadruple screw; speed 20 knots
Passengers 284 first class, 100 second class, 808 Asiatic steerage
Demise Attacked by Japanese planes in 1942

Canadian Pacific's new flagship, *Empress of Asia*, was completed in May 1913. On 14 June the white hulled liner set sail from Liverpool on her maiden voyage to the Mediterranean, then via the Suez Canal to Hong Kong, Shanghai and Yokohama, arriving at Victoria on 31 August. Twelve months later, on 2 August 1914, she was requisitioned at Hong Kong for service as an armed merchant cruiser in Chinese waters and the Indian Ocean. Like her sister, *Empress of Russia*, *Empress of Asia* was returned to Canadian Pacific in March 1916 and placed back on transpacific duty. However, towards the end of the war in May 1918 she was called on again as a troop transport, and served as such until February 1919. Handed back to Canadian Pacific,

Above *Canadian Pacific's flagship from 1913 to 1919,* Empress of Asia (Canadian Pacific).

Below *The masculine-looking Smoking Room of* Empress of Asia (Canadian Pacific).

Empress of Asia had a black hull from 1919 to 1926 (Canadian Pacific).

Empress of Asia was given an overhaul and her capacity was revised to 350 first class, 70 second class, 90 third class and 728 steerage class passengers.

Now sporting a black hull (which was repainted white in 1926), *Empress of Asia* returned to service in 1919, though not as flagship, as that title now went to *Empress of France*. Her job was to make fast transpacific passages, and in July 1924 she sailed from Yokohama to William Head, British Columbia, Canada, in 8 days 14 hours 48 minutes at an average speed of 20.2 knots. Calling at Shanghai, Hong Kong and occasionally Manila, *Empress of Asia* was able to undertake six round trips annually. Unfortunately her spotless record was shattered on 11 January 1926 in a collison outside Shanghai with the British

freighter *Tung Shing*, which sank with no loss of life. Following minor repairs, *Empress of Asia* emerged with a white hull.

When the Second World War erupted in Europe, *Empress of Asia* was in Shanghai. She sailed two days later for Vancouver, arriving in October 1939. A six-inch anti-submarine gun and a three-inch high-angle anti-aircraft gun were fitted to the liner and under the guidance of the Royal Navy she resumed her transpacific run.

When *Empress of Asia* arrived at Vancouver on 11 January 1941, concluding her 307th crossing, it proved to be the last scheduled Pacific sailing by a Canadian Pacific 'Empress'. Within a month she was requisitioned for service as a troop-ship, leaving Vancouver on 13 February 1941 for England via the Panama Canal. After conversion, she sailed from Liverpool in April 1941 for Freetown, Cape Town, Durban and Suez, returning to Liverpool by the same route. Her next departure from Liverpool was on 12 November to Cape Town, Bombay and Singapore. On 4 February 1942, the convoy was sighted by Japanese aircraft. The next day, while off Singapore, *Empress of Asia* was attacked by 27 enemy planes. For one and a half hours she was mercilessly besieged until, with five direct bomb-hits and 19 dead, she caught fire and sank nine miles from Keppel Harbour.

In 1951, International Salvage Association Ltd purchased the underwriters' rights to remove the wreck, a process which it started in 1952.

Empress of Canada

Builders Fairfield Shipbuilding & Engineering Co Ltd, 1922
Specification 21,517 gross tons, 650 ft (198 m) long, 77 ft (24 m) wide
Machinery Geared turbines; twin screw; speed 18 knots

Passengers 488 first class, 106 second class, 238 third class, 926 steerage
Demise Torpedoed in 1943

In 1919, Fairfield received an order for a 21,000-ton liner whose machinery could be converted to burn coal should the need arise. Launched by Mrs G. M. Bosworth, wife of the chairman, in a ceremony held on 17 August 1920, *Empress of Canada* was completed and handed over to CP in May 1922. On the fifth of that month she left Falmouth on her maiden voyage to Hong Kong and Vancouver via the Suez Canal. Planned welcoming ceremonies were cancelled in Vancouver and Victoria when it was learned that a case of smallpox had been detected on board. A year later, she broke all existing records when she steamed the 4,262 miles from Yokohama to Vancouver in 8 days 10 hours 53 minutes at an average speed of 20.6 knots.

Empress of Canada was a more lavishly furnished vessel than her fleet-mates, *Empress of*

Empress of Canada made the first round-the-world cruise for CP in 1924 (Canadian Pacific).

Empress of Canada was painted white in 1929 (Canadian Pacific).

Russia and *Empress of Asia*. Responsible for her interiors was the London firm of George Crawley & Partners. On A-Deck they created a gallery 110 ft long panelled in Honduras mahogany. This gallery gave access to all the principal first class public rooms on A-Deck, the most notable of which was the oak-panelled smoking-room that led into the verandah cafe. For the physically minded there was a 30 ft swimming-pool and a fully equipped gymnasium, both on D-Deck. Cabins were modestly decorated, with 40 being given private baths and toilets.

Empress of Canada undertook Canadian Pacific's first round-the-world cruise on 30 January 1924, when she departed from New York for the Mediterranean, Suez Canal, India, South-east Asia, China, Japan and North America. Three years later, in March 1927, she was involved in a collision with the Japanese steamer *Jinsho Maru* at Shanghai; both vessels suffered minor damage.

On 1 November 1928, *Empress of Canada* left Vancouver for the Clyde via the Suez to be re-engined by Fairfield. She emerged from the

Empress of Canada was painted white in 1929 (Canadian Pacific).

shipyard with a white hull and new geared turbines giving her a speed of 21 knots. She returned to service on 28 August 1929, making one round trip to Canada, after which she was dispatched from Southampton on 18 September for New York, Panama and Vancouver, returning to take up her former run on the transpacific route. *Empress of Canada* was involved in another collision on 7 November 1932, with the Japanese vessel *Yetai Maru* during a voyage from Kobe to Shanghai. As in the previous collision, both ships sustained minor damage.

Empress of Canada was requisitioned at Hong Kong on 29 November 1939 by the Ministry of War Transport, having completed 200 Pacific crossings. After conversion to a troop transport, she departed from Hong Kong as HMT X5 on 8 December for New Zealand, where she embarked troops for Suez. Returning to Sydney, she joined the 'multi-million dollar' convoy of seven liners—*Empress of Britain, Empress of Japan, Queen Mary, Aquitania, Mauretania* and *Andes*—that sailed on 5 May 1940 for South Africa and the Middle East. *Empress of Canada* called at South Africa then continued north, arriving on the Clyde in June. Four trips to the Middle East followed and then she went north to participate in 'Operation Gauntlet', the Allied raid on Spitzbergen that took place in August 1941. Her next mission was a circumnavigation of the earth calling at South Africa, Ceylon, Singapore, New Zealand, Panama, the United States and Canada before reaching home on 22 March 1942. A long trooping voyage to Bombay was next, followed by two short trips to Oran to supply troops for the North Africa landings.

Her end came in the South Atlantic on a voyage from Durban to England. On 13 March 1943, at 11.54 pm, *Empress of Canada* was struck on the starboard side by a torpedo fired from the Italian sumbarine *Leonardo da Vinci*. All electric power was immediately lost and the ship took on a list. At 12.50 am another torpedo was fired, finishing off the dying liner. *Empress of Canada* sank in position 1° 13′S-9°57′W, taking with her 392 souls.

Empress of Australia

(Tirpitz, Empress of China)

Builders Vulcan AG, Stettin, 1914
Specifications 21,860 tons; 615 ft (187 m) long, 75 ft (23 m) wide
Machinery Steam turbines; twin screw; speed 16.5 knots
Passengers 400 first class, 165 second class, 350 third-class, 650 steerage
Demise Scrapped in 1952

Hamburg-America's answer to Hamburg-South America Line's *Cap Trafalgar* and *Cap Polonio* was the construction of three ships for its South American service. First to be launched was *Admiral von Tirpitz* on 20 December 1913, followed by *Johann Heinrich Burchard* in February 1914 and *William O'Swald* in March 1914. Two

Empress of Australia *sporting a black hull* (Canadian Pacific).

months after being launched, *Admiral von Tirpitz's* name was changed to *Tirpitz*.

If a shot had not been fired in Sarajevo, Hamburg-America would have had a handsome trio of first-class liners plying the southern hemisphere, but once the global conflict erupted, work on *Tirpitz* was suspended for the duration of the war. In 1919 the 19,300-ton *Tirpitz* was handed over to Britain and sent to Hull where the Ministry of Shipping used her briefly as a troop transport. In 1920 she made several voyages under Cunard management, eventually being laid up at Immingham in February 1921. On 25 July 1921, *Tirpitz* was purchased by Canadian Pacific from the Reparations Commission and renamed *Empress of China* three days later. On 8 August she was sent to AG Vulcan at Hamburg for a refit; the work was completed at John Brown on Clydebank in May 1922, and the next month Canadian Pacific changed its 21,860-ton liner's name to *Empress of Australia*.

A unique feature of this transpacific lady was her machinery. Two sets of impulse-reaction turbines drove her twin screw through a form of hydraulic transmission known as the Fottinger Hydraulic Transformer. This experimental drive had the merit of being reversible, thus obviating the need for astern turbines. In service, however, it proved to be inefficient and its inherent slip reduced the ship's speed of 17.5 knots to a little more than 15.5 knots.

Empress of Australia's first sailing under the chequered house flag was made on 16 June 1922 when she left Glasgow for Vancouver, sailing via the Panama Canal. She arrived on 19 July and joined her first class consorts *Empress of Russia*, *Empress of Asia* and *Empress of Canada* on the transpacific service, calling at Yokohama, Shanghai, Hong Kong and Manila. Although she proved to be a bit slow and her fuel consumption was high, her interior appointments were in tune with her running mates.

Empress of Australia had a straight stem, counter stern and three funnels, the after one used only as an engine-room ventilator. Following the German fashion of the time (1913), the uptakes of her other two funnels were divided, providing for the creation of a series of magnificent public rooms. The most notable was the main lounge on A-Deck. Its pillarless chamber roof and dome were built on the cantilever principle, while the walls and ceiling were finished in green and gilt, with furniture done in satinwood. The dining-room had a large central dome and was decorated in Louis XVI style with mahogany furniture; an orchestra gallery at the after end provided musical selections at mealtimes.

As *Empress of Australia* was casting off from her wharf at Yokohama on 1 September 1923, the first series of shocks were felt of the great earthquake that was to devastate the port city. The first shocks shattered the pier whence she had departed and swirled her through the harbour. She was brought under control and Captain S. Robinson ordered the lifeboats to be lowered to rescue survivors from the land. *Empress of Canada* arrived on Monday 3 September on her normal schedule and provided her sistership with additional stores and offered to take some refugees to Kobe. In an attempt to move astern on 4 September, *Empress of Australia's* screws became entangled in the anchor chains of another vessel. Unmanoeuvrable, she collided with a Japanese ship and continued to drift out of control with over 2,000 people aboard, heading towards a burning oilfield. The captain sent out an SOS and the Dutch tanker *Iris* responded. She towed the 'Empress' to open water from where her boats continued the rescue work. Filled to capacity, she sailed for Kobe on September 8 where she was relieved by the arrival of *Empress of Russia*. Later, Captain Robinson was invested with the CBE and awarded the silver medal of the Order of St John of Jerusalem.

Empress of Australia continued in Pacific service until 1926. On 4 August she sailed from Hong Kong via the Suez to Fairfield at Glasgow where her troublesome slow engines were replaced with new Parsons turbines and her passenger capacity was restructured to 400 first class, 150 second class and 630 third class, giving her a new gross tonnage of 21,833.

Flying the Prince of Wales' standard, *Empress of Australia* departed from Southampton on 25 June 1927 for Cherbourg and Quebec, her new route. On board was the Prince of Wales, Prince George and Prime Minister Stanley Baldwin,

Right Empress of Australia *during one of her early
transits through the Panama
Canal* (Canadian Pacific).

Below *Following her 1926
refit, the now white hulled*
Empress of Australia *was
placed on the North Atlantic
run* (Canadian Pacific).

who were visiting Canada to take part in celebrations commemorating the 60th year of Confederation. Later in the year, on 2 December, she left New York on the first of four world cruises.

During the lean economic years following the Depression, *Empress of Australia* was employed on a number of cruises from both Southampton and New York to the Mediterranean, Scandinavia and the West Indies. To capture her share of trans-Atlantic passengers during the summer months, her accommodation was restyled in 1936 to 387 cabin class, 394 tourist class and 358 third class. For the fortunate few who could afford a summer vacation in Europe, one-way fares in 1936 were $163 (£33) cabin class, $117.50 (£24) tourist class and $84.50 (£17) third class for a six-day voyage.

Honour was bestowed on *Empress of Australia* when she was selected as the ship on which the King and Queen would sail to Canada. On 6 May 1939, with the Royal Standard flown at the foremast, the Admiralty flag on the main and the white ensign on the stern, Their Majesties King George VI and Queen Elizabeth and their party of 69 embarked at Portsmouth for their voyage to Quebec. For the occasion, the smoking-room was converted into a private dining-room with tables and chairs borrowed from the Royal Yacht.

Four months after the royal voyage *Empress of Australia* departed from Quebec on 2 September 1939 on her last commercial voyage to Southampton. In all, she had completed 83 round trips on the North Atlantic.

In England, she was requisitioned as a troopship and was utilized world-wide. Armed with a three-inch high angle gun and a few machine guns, *Empress of Australia* departed for Colombo and then Halifax. Subsequent voyages were made to Singapore, Norway (for the Norwegian campaigns), Iceland, Durban, North Africa, Oran and Murmansk. After the conflict, she was

engaged in reparation work and the transport of civil servants to colonial posts in India and Hong Kong. Her end came on 7 May 1952 when she was sold to British Iron & Steel Corporation for scrapping; three days later, she arrived at Inverkeithing to be broken up.

Empress of Japan

(Empress of Scotland, Scotland, Hanseatic)

Builders Fairfield Shipbuilding & Engineering Co Ltd, Glasgow, 1930
Specifications 26,032 gross tons; 666 ft (203 m) long, 83 ft (25 m) wide
Machinery Geared turbines; twin screw; speed 21 knots
Passengers 399 first class, 164 second class, 100 third class, 510 steerage
Demise Burned in 1966

Ordered in 1928, Canadian Pacific's future flagship was ready for launching in December 1929. Performing the honours was Mrs Peacock, wife of the director of CP. Within a year, on 8 June 1930, *Empress of Japan* was completed. Her maiden voyage was across the Atlantic to Quebec; she departed from Liverpool on 14 June 1930, returning to Southampton in July. *Empress of Japan* was dispatched on 12 July to the Orient and Vancouver via the Suez Canal under the command of the veteran Captain Robinson, and she quickly established herself as the fastest liner in the Pacific by steaming from Yokohama to Vancouver in 8 days 6 hours 27 minutes, taking the record from *Empress of Canada*, and upon her arrival at Vancouver a banquet was held on board to celebrate the occasion.

Empress of Japan joined her fleet-mates, Empress of Russia, *Empress of Asia* and *Empress of Canada*, in providing fast, comfortable Pacific passages. One-way 1933 summer fares in dollars

Left *The only liner to be a flagship and 'speed queen' twice was* Empress of Japan *(Canadian Pacific).*

Right *The first class Dining Room of* Empress of Japan *(Canadian Pacific).*

(pounds) for *Empress of Japan* from Vancouver/ Victoria to Far East ports were as follows:

Vancouver to:	Days	First	Tourist	Third	Servants	
					European	Oriental
Honolulu	5	110 (27)	85 (21)	65 (16)	110 (27)	50 (12)
Yokohama	14	310 (77)	190 (47)	80 (20)	248 (62)	55 (14)
Shanghai	16	356 (89)	215 (54)	110 (27)	285 (71)	80 (20)
Hong Kong	19	385 (96)	230 (57)	112.50 (28)	308 (77)	82.50 (21)
Manila	22	385 (96)	230 (57)	120 (30)	308 (77)	90 (22)

Honolulu was added due to the speed of 'Empresses' *Japan* and *Canada*; though 1,500 miles out of the way, the ships were able to call at Honolulu and still arrive at Vancouver a day before the American and Japanese competition reached San Francisco, a shorter distance.

Accommodation on *Empress of Japan* was on a modern scale, with an emphasis on spaciousness, though not for third class or steerage. Her public rooms were situated on Promenade Deck and

consisted of a palm court, a full-width ballroom furnished with red and black lacquered furniture, a lounge with a large oval dome and a long gallery on the port side panelled in ash and walnut. Elevators transported first class passengers between her seven decks.

Empress of Japan was called upon to serve her country as a troop transport on 26 November 1939 at Hong Kong. Sporting a coat of grey paint, she departed from Hong Kong on 2 December for Sydney to embark 773 troops for Port Said. She returned to Sydney and in May 1940 joined convoy US3 that included *Empress of Britain*, *Empress of Canada*, *Aquitania*, *Mauretania*, *Andes* and *Queen Mary*. When the convoy reached Cape Town, *Empress of Japan* disembarked her troops, took aboard the Chinese crew from *Empress of Canada* and sailed for Hong Kong. On 3 August she sailed for the Clyde by way of Australia, New Zealand, Bombay, Suez and Durban, then three voyages were undertaken to Singapore in January, June and October 1941.

Pearl Harbor was attacked by Japan in December 1941, but for unknown reasons it was not until October 1942 that the British changed the ship's name to the less sensitive *Empress of Scotland*. During the years 1943 and 1944, she was used on the Atlantic shuttle, sailing from either Halifax, New York or Newport News to either Liverpool or Casablanca. Her final three years of government service were spent on voyages to Australia and Bombay. During her eight and a half years of war service, the 'Empress' steamed more than 720,000 miles and, working under the most strenuous circumstances, spent only 125 days in repair yards—a testament to British shipbuilding. Equally lauded were her captains. There were only two during her entire war service; one was Captain Thomas, who was staff commander in 1939, promoted to captain in 1940.

Empress of Scotland was decommissioned and handed back to Canadian Pacific on 8 May 1948. Taken into Fairfield, she was given a thorough overhaul and refitted for trans-Atlantic service. The Promenade Deck was enclosed with windows and her capacity was reduced from 1,173 to 663—458 first class and 205 tourist class passengers. At 26,313 gross tons, she again served as Canadian Pacific's flagship until her retirement.

Painted all in white, *Empress of Scotland* departed from Liverpool on her first trans-Atlantic voyage on 9 May 1950, for Greenock and Quebec. The next month she accomplished a westbound crossing in 4 days 14 hours 42 minutes and eastbound in 4 days 23 hours 30 minutes, becoming not only the largest but also the fastest liner on the St Lawrence service. In

Left *With her new name,* Empress of Scotland *was CP's flagship and record-breaker after the war* (Canadian Pacific).

Right *The cosy tourist class lounge of* Empress of Scotland (Canadian Pacific).

Below *The comfortable first class lounge of* Empress of Scotland (Canadian Pacific).

German Atlantic's Hanseatic (Richard Morse Collection).

December 1950, she departed from New York on her first cruise, and the company's first post-war cruise. In all, she sailed on seven Caribbean cruises during that first season, and established a winter pattern that continued for the next seven years. In May 1952, her Canadian terminal was extended to Montreal, and in order that she might negotiate the bridges, her masts were shortened. On 12 November 1952, she made a special call at Portugal Cove, Newfoundland, to embark their Royal Highnesses Princess Elizabeth and the Duke of Edinburgh to complete their voyage to Liverpool.

Competition on the Canadian run was stiff. When tighter Canadian immigration controls were imposed, a decrease in passenger loads was expected, and *Empress of Scotland* was therefore withdrawn from service. She made her last transatlantic voyage when she sailed from Liverpool on 8 November 1957 for Quebec and Montreal. Upon her return to Liverpool she was laid up, having completed some 91 round trips and 29 cruises.

On 1 January 1958, *Empress of Scotland* was dry-docked at Belfast. Thirteen days later, she was sold for £1 million to the newly-formed German company, Hamburg-Atlantic Line. They renamed her *Scotland*, and she sailed from Belfast on 19 January for Howaldtswerke shipyard at Hamburg.

There she was extensively refitted and refurbished and, with a new steamlined black hull, 30,030 tons and twin funnels, *Hanseatic* emerged. A new bow made her 673 ft (205 m) long, and outdoor swimming-pool was added to the Boat Deck and the interior was made completely air-conditioned. Space was provided for 85 first class and 1,167 tourist class passengers, all in cabins with private facilities.

Hanseatic departed from Cuxhaven on her first transatlantic voyage on 19 July 1958. En route she called at Le Havre and Southampton before proceeding to New York. In the spring of 1961, her funnels were extended with a 'stove-pipe' flue configuration supported by a domed skeleton.

Hanseatic's itinerary rarely changed. Late spring, summer and autumn she was engaged in transatlantic sailings, and during the winter she was sent cruising from either Cuxhaven, New York or Port Everglades, being one of the pioneers in sailing from that Florida port. In the summer of 1962, Hamburg-Atlantic initiated an annual North Cape summer cruise from Germany.

At 7.30 am on 7 September 1966, a fire started in the engine-room when diesel oil leaking from a ruptured fuel line or a faulty gasket reached the ship's hot engines. Flames quickly engulfed the two engine-rooms and spread upwards, undetected, through hidden vents to the five passenger decks. Luckily only three of the 425 passengers were on board the vessel, which was scheduled to depart at 11.30 am; the sailing was cancelled and the damage assessed. Too costly to repair, *Hanseatic* was first laid up in New York, then towed to Hamburg by the ocean-going tugs *Atlantic* and *Pacific*, where she was sold on 2 December 1966 to Eisen & Metall AG, Hamburg, to be broken up.

CP's flagship Empress of Britain *on a cruise* (National Archives, Washington DC).

Empress of Britain

Builders John Brown & Company Ltd, Clydebank, 1931
Specifications 42,348 gross tons; 760 ft (232 m) long, 97 ft (30 m) wide
Machinery Geared turbines; quadruple screw; speed 24 knots
Passengers 465 first class, 260 tourist class, 470 third class
Demise Torpedoed in 1940

Deciding it was time to replace the ageing *Empress of Scotland*, built in 1905 as Hamburg-America's *Kaiser Auguste Victoria*, Canadian Pacific placed an order with John Brown & Company for the largest liner to be built in

Britain since the White Star liner *Britannic* in 1915. *Empress of Britain* was laid down on 28 November 1928 and launched in a ceremony performed by HRH The Prince of Wales on 11 June 1930. The event was broadcast throughout the Commonwealth and the United States, and became one of the first events to be so transmitted. In under a year, the giant was completed. Following trails and open house, the 'Empress' departed on 27 May 1931 on her maiden voyage from Southampton to Cherbourg and Quebec. Her fastest westbound passage was accomplished in October 1933 when she steamed from Bishop Rock to Belle Isle in 3 days 2 hours. Her

eastbound record passage was performed in August 1934 between Belle Isle and Bishop Rock in 3 days 1 hour 36 minutes at an average speed of 25.08 knots. On average, her passage occupied six days.

Empress of Britain embodied many epitaphs. She was the largest vessel ever to sail for Canadian Pacific, she was the largest and fastest ship ever placed on the Canadian route and she became the first liner to be fitted with ship-to-shore radio telephones. She was readily distinguishable by her straight stem, cruiser stern, white hull and three huge buff funnels, the aftermost of which was a dummy used as an engine-room ventilat-

Left *The launching of* Empress of Britain *on 11 June 1930* (Canadian Pacific).

Below *A hearty* bon voyage *for* Empress of Britain (National Archives, Washington DC).

ing air intake; each funnel was 35 ft (11 m) in diameter and 68 ft (21 m) high. With a blue line around her hull and a green water-line, *Empress of Britain* made an unforgettable sight, and at night her three mammoth stacks were illuminated by floodlights.

Canadian Pacific spared no expense in fitting out its flagship. On D-Deck was the lovely dining-room, occupying the full length of the ship. Above on Promenade Deck was a string of lavishly appointed public rooms. The Empress Ballroom, which doubled as a cinema, was designed by Sir John Lavery, and its outstanding feature was a large dome on which was a representation of the heavens on the night of the launch. The Knickerbocker Bar contained a panoramic mural called 'The Legend of the Cocktail'. Charles Allom used a variety of traditional woods to execute the Mayfair Lounge, while his colleague, Edmund Dulac, used Chinese lacquer vases and Chinese motifs on the walls and furnishings to decorate the Cathay Lounge. For physical recreation, there was an Olympian Pool situated on F-Deck, water for which flowed from a large turtle carved in Portland stone and inlaid with blue mosaic. Alongside the pool were the Turkish baths and massage rooms. Elsewhere on board were two

gymnasiums, a squash court and a full-size tennis court on the sport deck. These luxuries could be enjoyed in 1936 for a minimum of $236 (£48) first class. A deluxe suite with two bedrooms, sitting-room, sun verandah, bathroom and box-room cost $1,244 (£252). However, for those not wanting such luxury, comfortable accommodation was available at $130.50 (£26) second class and $87.50 (£18) third class.

Empress of Britain spent her first season plying the North Atlantic. She then headed for New York to undertake what was to become an annual event—circumnavigating the world. On 21 November 1931 she left New York with 400 lucky passengers on her first world cruise, a 146-day affair with tariffs starting at $2,138 (£440). Her 1936 world cruise lasted 130 days, visited 31 ports in 23 countries and cost, including shore excursions, a minimum of $2,150 (£445). Both rates were for an inside cabin with no private facilities. For these cruises her two outer propellors were made detachable, giving her a crusing speed of 18 knots. Further, space was provided on deck for the installation of a portable outdoor swimming-pool. When *Empress of Britain* passed through both the Suez and Panama canals in 1931, she became the largest ship to do so, although her Panama Canal

The first class Dining Room of Empress of Britain) (Canadian Pacific).

The tourist class Dining Room on board Empress of Britain (Canadian Pacific).

honour was eclipsed in February 1939 when the *Bremen* sailed through.

During *Empress of Britain's* brief ten-year career, she was involved in two incidents, both in 1935. On 16 May, while passing through the Gatun Lock in the Panama Canal she scraped her side and received minor damage. On 16 June, heading east under thick fog off Magdalen Islands in the Gulf of St Lawrence, she rammed the collier *Kafiristan*. The latter was badly damaged and set on fire; *Empress of Britain* waited alongside until *Beaverford* arrived and towed the *Kafiristan* to Sydney, Nova Scotia. The 'Empress' then proceeded to Southampton where the hole in her starboard bow was repaired.

The Royal Family chose *Empress of Britain* to return from their Canadian tour. On 16 June 1939, HM King George VI and Queen Elizabeth, along with their retinue, boarded the ship at Conception Bay, St Johns, Newfoundland, for their voyage home to Southampton.

Within three months, on 2 September 1939, *Empress of Britain* commenced her 100th voyage from Southampton with her largest passenger list—1,143. At Quebec she was painted grey and laid up awaiting requisitioning orders. They came in November and she sailed for the Clyde on 10 December as part of a convoy from Canada. Having completed three trips across the Atlantic, the 'Empress' sailed in March 1940 for Wellington, New Zealand. She then joined the great convoy of luxury liners which left Sydney on 5 May 1940 and sailed to Cape Town, whence she continued back to the Clyde. Her next departure, from Liverpool, occurred on 6 August for Suez via Cape Town; she travelled independently of escorts. That voyage was followed by a transatlantic crossing to Canada.

En route back to England from Canads on 26 October 1940, some 60 nautical miles north-west of Ireland, *Empress of Britain* was spotted by German aircraft whose pilots proceeded to bomb her and set her afire. A British flying boat spotted the burning ship and summoned warships to the scene, but she was aflame from stem to stern and her complement of 643 persons took to the boats to be rescued by the various naval vessels summoned by the flying boat. Deemed salvageable, the British tugs *Marauder* and *Thames* took the 'Empress' in tow, but the next day *Empress of Britain* was torpedoed and sunk by German submarine U-32 in position 55°16'N-09°50'W. Considering the circumstances, it is fortunate that the casualties were limited to 49 dead. *Empress of Britain* became the third largest ship to rest on the ocean floor, the others being *Titanic* and *Britannic*.

Above Lutetia *was flagship for only 28 days* (Henry W. Uhle, SSHSA Collection).

Below Lutetia *at Rio de Janeiro* (Henry W. Uhle, SSHSA Collection).

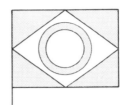

Compagnie de Navigation Sud Atlantique

Lutetia

Builders Chantiers et Ateliers de St Nazaire (Penhoët), St Nazaire, 1913
Specifications 14,561 gross tons; 600 ft (183 m) long, 64 ft (20 m) wide
Machinery Triple expansion engines; quadruple screw; speed 20 knots
Passengers 300 first class, 110 second class, 80 third class, 600 steerage
Demise Scrapped in 1938

Sud Atlantique commissioned a handsome trio of mail steamers between 1913 and 1920 for their South American service. The first to be launched, on 23 March 1913, was *Lutetia*. Completed seven months later, *Lutetia*, with a red cockerel painted on each funnel, was ready to set sail on her maiden voyage on 1 November 1913, proceeding from Bordeaux to Brazil and Argentina. Her triple-expansion engines and low-pressure steam turbines gave her an average speed of 18.7 knots, making her the fastest ship on the South American run.

After leaving Lisbon on her homeward maiden voyage, *Lutetia* collided with and sank the Greek cargo steamer *Dimitrios*. *Lutetia* was obliged to return to Lisbon, where her passengers disembarked and proceeded to their European destinations by train. After temporary repairs were made, *Lutetia* sailed for St Nazaire for permanent repairs.

In August 1914, *Lutetia* became a troop trans-port, and sixteen months later she was fitted out as an auxiliary cruiser. In 1916 she briefly served as a hospital ship, before reverting back to a troop transport. Released from naval service in 1919, she was refitted as a passenger ship at La Seyne. Her tonnage was increased from 14,561 to 14,654 and her capacity was restyled to accommodate 460 first class, 130 second class, 90 third class and 450 steerage passengers. *Lutetia* resumed her sailings on 2 October 1920 and was joined at the end of the month by her sister ship *Massilia*, and between them they provided a monthly express service from Bordeaux to Buenos Aires.

Lutetia was taken out of service in 1927 and taken to Penhoët at St Nazaire to be converted to an oil burner. During a storm on the night of 15 June, the liner heeled over and sank. She was, however, raised on 23 June, work was completed by November and she resumed service on 19 November. *Lutetia* suffered another accident in March 1928, when she collided with the Lamport & Holt steamer *Balzac* at Buenos Aires. Both were damaged in collision, resulting in a delayed voyage home.

Adjusting to the times, *Lutetia's* accommodation figures were altered again in 1930 to 212 first class, 114 second class, 86 third class and 500 steerage passengers. When the United States tightened its immigration laws, Europeans seeking a new land in which to settle turned to South America, but the depression hurt even the South American trade. In August 1931, *Lutetia* was laid up at Bordeaux, and in November 1937 she was

" LE GALLIA ", Croiseur auxiliaire
Coulé dans la Méditerranée, le 4 octobre 1916

sold for breaking up and left for Blyth on 28 January 1938.

Gallia

Builders Forges et Chantiers de la Méditerranée, La Seyne, 1913
Specifications 14,966 gross tons; 600 ft (183 m) long, 62 ft (19 m) wide
Machinery Triple expansion engines; triple screw; speed 20 knots
Passengers 300 first class, 106 second class, 80 third class, 600 steerage
Demise Torpedoed in 1916

The second of the trio of mail express steamers for Sud Atlantique was *Gallia*, launched on 26 March 1913. Completed in October, she was ready to depart from Bordeaux on her maiden voyage to Buenos Aires on 29 November 1913. Unlike her sister *Lutetia*, *Gallia* was a triple screw liner and there were problems with her engines. Therefore, on her arrival at Bordeaux she was taken back to Le Seyne for engine work and also some alterations to increase her first class capacity; she resumed service in January 1914.

Gallia was summoned to military service in August 1914 as an auxiliary cruiser in the French Navy. Later she was converted into a troop transport. Carrying 2,350 troops to Salonica on 4 October 1916, *Gallia* was sighted 35 nautical miles west of Sardinia by German submarine U-35. The submarine fired torpedoes into the liner and she sank within 15 minutes. Six hundred troops were rescued the next day by the passing French cruiser *Chateaurenault*.

Massilia

Builders Forges et Chantiers de la Méditerranée, La Seyne, 1920
Specifications 15,147 gross tons; 600 ft (183 m) long, 64 ft (20 m) wide
Machinery Triple expansion engines; quadruple screw; speed 20 knots
Passengers 464 first class, 129 second class, 98 third class, 350 steerage
Demise Scuttled in 1944

Massilia was the last of the trio ordered by Sud Atlantique in 1912. Launched on 30 April 1914, work was then suspended for the duration of the war. Construction resumed in 1919 and *Massilia* was completed in September 1920. Sud Atlantique took delivery of its new flagship on 8 October and, following the celebrations, the new liner was made ready. Her three funnels were painted in the company's new colours of buff with black tops and she departed from Bordeaux on 30 October 1920 for South America. Her transatlantic crossing of 9 days 19 hours between Lisbon and Rio de Janeiro was a record, snatching the honour of the fastest liner on the route from her sister ship *Lutetia*. *Massilia* then settled down with *Lutetia* to provide a monthly service between Bordeaux and Buenos Aires.

Sud Atlantique considered it economically feasible to convert their ships to oil firing; *Lutetia* was first, and once she returned to service, it was *Massilia's* turn in 1928. The work was carried out by Chantiers et Ateliers at St Nazaire. In the process her bridge deck was altered and her tonnage increased to 15,363. Two years later, her passenger figures were adjusted to 231 first class, 71 second class, 88 third class and 456 steerage.

Massilia was joined in 1931 by her giant running mate *L'Atlantique* and the two maintained the Sud Atlantique presence in the southern hemisphere for two years, after which *L'Atlantique* was burned, leaving *Massilia* to carry on unaided by a suitable consort.

In April 1940, *Massilia* was requisitioned as a troop transport and on 18 June she sailed from Bordeaux with 150 members of the French Parliament for Casablanca. She then sailed to Liverpool to collect a number of French soldiers who had escaped from Dunkirk and landed them at Toulon. She was then laid up at Marseilles and in due course became an accommodation ship for the Germans. In their retreat from France in 1944, the Germans scuttled *Massilia* off the Basin Mirabeau in order to block the harbour. After the war the wreck was salvaged and scrapped.

Above left Gallia *sailed for Sud Atlantique for only a few months before being torpedoed in 1916* (Alex Shaw, SSHSA Collection).

Right *The flagship of Sud Atlantique for 11 years was* Massilia (Richard Morse Collection).

Right *Sud Atlantique flagship* L'Atlantique *before her funnels were heightened* (Richard Morse Collection).

L'Atlantique

Builders Chantiers et Ateliers de St Nazaire
(Penhoët), St Nazaire, 1931
Specifications 42,512 gross tons; 744 ft (227 m)
long, 92 ft (28 m) wide
Machinery Geared steam turbines; quadruple
screw; speed 21 knots
Passengers 414 first class, 158 second class, 584
third class
Demise Burned in 1933.

The largest ship ever commissioned for Sud
Atlantique was *L'Atlantique*, whose keel was laid
down on 28 November 1928. She was launched
on 15 April 1930, and was ready for service
seventeen months later. *L'Atlantique* was not
only Sud Atlantique's flagship, but the largest
built for the South American trade, and, because
of her size, the company found it more desirable
for departures and arrivals to take place at Pauillac, 30 miles downstream from Bordeaux. During her time she was also the fastest on the route,
her speed record not being surpassed until 1966

Left *The giant bow*
of L'Atlantique *(Chantier
de l'Atlantique, Saint-
Nazaire).*

Right *'La Rue de la Paix',
150 yards long, aboard*
L'Atlantique *(Illustrated
London News).*

Right *The Grand Salon
of* L'Atlantique *certainly
rivalled those of other liners
on the North Atlantic (Illustrated London News).*

by Costa's *Eugenio C. L'Atlantique* was completed in September and departed from Pauillac on 29 September 1931, for her maiden dash to Rio and Buenos Aires.

The exterior of *L'Atlantique* was very traditional. She had a black hull with a white line around it, plenty of promenade deck space for the tropics, two masts, a cruiser stern, luffing davits (quite a surprise for 1931) and three huge bluff funnels with black tops, the aftermost being a dummy. It was in her interiors, however, that *L'Atlantique* broke with tradition. What *Ile de France* did for the North Atlantic, *L'Atlantique* accomplished in the South. Gone were the re-creations of pretty period castles and palaces. Instead, *L'Atlantique* was one of the most modern ships in the world. Like *Vaterland* and *Bismarck*, the uptakes from the engine room were divided so as to give a long unrestricted vista through the centre of the ship. The central avenue was known as 'La Rue de la Paix' and was 450 ft long and three decks high with rows of luxury shops on both sides. A luxurious pillar-free Grand Salon decorated in art deco style was provided for first class passengers, as well as a chapel, children's playroom, tennis court (between the second and third funnels) and a swimming-pool forward of the mainmast. To keep the fumes and soot from troubling the passengers, Sud Atlantique heightened *L'Atlantique's* funnels in 1932.

At 3.30 am on 4 January 1933, during a positioning voyage to Le Havre to be dry-docked, a fire broke out in cabin 232 on E-Deck. The flames and smoke spread rapidly through the ship, forcing the crew to abandon her; 17 lives were lost in the havoc. For two days the fire burned out of control and the ship drifted helplessly in the English Channel towards the Dorset coast of Portland Bill. Finally, on 6 January, *L'Atlantique* was taken in two to Cherbourg by French, Dutch and German tugs.

Once she was safely tied up, a court battle ensued between the underwriters and Sud Atlantique. The owners claimed the ship was a constructive total loss and claimed her value at £2 million. The underwriters claimed that Harland & Wolff's estimate of the complete repair job (£1,250,000) was lower than the owner's claim. The company finally won their case, and *L'Atlantique* languished at Cherbourg until she was sold for scrap to Smith & Houston Ltd, Port Glasgow, in 1936.

Above *After the fire, the collapsed decks of* L'Atlantique (Illustrated London News).

Right *The burnt-out* L'Atlantique *shown under tow from Cherbourg to the scrapyard* (Illustrated London News).

Above Paris, *aristocrat of the North Atlantic* (Author's Collection).

Below *The first class Smoke Room aboard the Paris* (Everett E. Viez, SSHSA Collection).

CIe GLe
TRANSATLANTIQUE

Compagnie Générale Transatlantique (French Line)

Paris

Builders Chantiers et Ateliers de St Nazaire (Penhoët), St Nazaire, 1921
Specifications 34,569 gross tons; 764 ft (233 m) long, 85 ft (26 m) wide
Machinery Steam turbines; quadruple screw; speed 21 knots
Passengers 563 first class, 460 second class, 1,092 third class
Demise Burned in 1939

On 1 November 1912, Compagnie Générale Transatlantique (French Line) entered into an agreement with the French government concerning the transatlantic mail service between Le Havre and New York. The agreement stipulated that French Line were to build four large vessels for this service within a five-year period, so, with a generous subsidy from the government, French Line commenced the building programme with the keel-laying of *Paris* in 1913.

Within a year, construction was suspended due to the outbreak of war. However, in order to free the slipway and enable the yard to construct tonnage for the Allied cause, work resumed and *Paris* was launched on 16 September 1916. She was towed to Quiberon Bay and laid up incomplete for the duration of the war.

Paris was completed in June 1921, and on 15 June France's largest liner and French Line's flagship left Le Havre for Plymouth and New York. *Paris*, her fleet-mate *France* and other smaller vessels were able to maintain a twice-weekly service betwen New York and Le Havre during the 1920s.

If not the largest liner to sail the Atlantic, *Paris* was certainly one of the best decorated, being affectionately known as 'The Aristocrat of the Atlantic'. Her interiors were in keeping with French Line's tradition of modelling its ships after French palaces and chateaux. There was a preoccupation with sweeping staircases leading into lounges and dining salons fit for royalty. The staircase in the main foyer was a series of swirling geometric patterns complete with illuminated dome, soaring arches and mosaic tiles modelled on the palaces of French North Africa. The grand salon was decorated in the style of the time of Marie Antoinette. The main dining-room had a glass cupola, balcony and mezzanine supported by columns of wrought iron. The railings around the balcony and the mirror-backed double staircase were of fine filigrees of wrought iron that featured a stork and a lion in a palm-fringed glade. This chamber gave credance to French Line's motto 'Low ceilings do not aid the appetite'. Finally, her *pièce de résistance* was the Salon de Thé. Instead of wood, the decorators opted for an illuminated dance floor of frosted glass panels lit from beneath. *Paris'* de luxe apartments were named after French provinces instead of being given numbers, and were decorated in a variety of styles and had windows. The ambience, personality and cuisine of *Paris* made her one of the favourites among artists, writers and musicians.

Paris was, however, plagued with ill-luck. In

1926 she collided with a pier at Le Havre that ripped a 66 ft (20 m) hole in her hull. She was repaired at the Wilton-Fijenoord yard at Rotterdam, becoming the largest ship to enter that port. On 15 October 1927, she ramed and sank the freighter *Bessengen* off Robbins Reef lighthouse in New York, resulting in six deaths. Encountering fog while proceeding to her pier on 6 April 1929, the Paris ran aground in New York's lower bay, then, less than two weeks later, on 18 April she was aground again off Eddystone lighthouse.

Her worst accident occurred on 20 August 1929 while she was sitting at Le Havre. A fire, believed to have been started deliberately, quickly spread from the third class area, destroying the passenger accommodation. French Line considered her worth repairing and she was towed to St Nazaire; in the process the opportunity was

Paris docked at New York; the other vessel is the San Diego (Everett E. Viez, SSHSA Collection).

taken to upgrade her accommodation. When *Paris* resumed service on 15 January 1930, her capacity had been revised to 560 first class, 530 second class and 844 third class passengers.

The Depression affected *Paris'* passenger loads, so to help fill berths, French Line dispatched her from France on her first Mediterranean cruise during the winter of 1931. When the sparkling *Normandie* took to the Atlantic in 1935, *Paris* was utilized more on cruises, with French Line giving serious consideration to converting her for full-time cruise service, although nothing came of the plan. When she undertook a cruise, she was usually leased to the well-known New York travel firm of Raymond-Whitcomb. It was with that firm that *Paris* made her last cruise from New York in June

1938, to France, Ireland and Scandinavia.

On 19 April 1939, *Paris* was again consumed by flames at Le Havre, and this time the blaze proved fatal. Fires started simultaneously in the ship's bakery and on two higher decks. The fire brigade was summoned and started pumping water into the liner; *Paris* eventually keeled over from the weight of the water and sank at her moorings, blocking *Normandie* in her repair berth. *Paris'* masts had to be cut immediately in order to let *Normandie* pass.

Soon afterwards, war erupted in Europe and salvage became less important, so the partially exposed hull and superstructure remained in the harbour. In November 1946, *Liberté* broke her moorings and collided with the wreck; when *Liberté* was moved, the remains of *Paris* were scrapped in 1947.

Ile de France

Builders Chantiers et Ateliers de St Nazaire (Penhoët), St Nazaire, 1927
Specifications 43,153 tons; 793 ft (241 m) long, 91 ft (28 m) wide
Machinery Geared turbines; quadruple screw; speed 23.5 knots
Passengers 537 first class, 603 second class, 646 third class
Demise Scrapped at Osaka in 1959

Not since the introduction of *Imperator* in 1913 was there such excitement in the maritime world over the arrival of a new ship. Hundreds of passenger vessels were introduced during the late 'teens and early 'twenties, yet sensationalism filled the air as the French Line publicist distributed brochures advertising its newest addition. What was this liner that was to become the epitome of the jazz age?

Abiding by their agreement of 1912, French Line ordered a second large vessel to run as consort to *Paris*. Originally the timetable called for large steamers to be delivered at five-year intervals—1916, 1921, 1926 and 1931—but war intervened and disrupted the plans. *Paris* had fulfilled the 1916 deadline, though she did not commence service until 1921, so this new steamer would satisfy the 1921 commitment.

Construction started on the new ship in 1924 at a time when French Line's turn-of-the-century vessels were beginning to show their age. Work progressed at a rapid pace, culminating on 14 March 1926, when, amidst rapturous speeches and applause, the new liner was christened *Ile de France* and sent down the slipways into the Loire River. Penhoët workers set to work fitting out the liner, while French Line's publicity de-

Ile de France (Compagnie Générale Maritime).

partment issued an elaborate gold-covered book-let devoted entirely to its new flagship. *Ile de France* was completed on 29 May 1927, and after successful trials was turned over to her new owners. On 5 June she docked at Le Havre and opened for public inspection. After receiving 'rave reviews', *Ile de France* commenced her maiden voyage on 22 June from Le Havre to Plymouth and New York with Captain Blancart in command.

At 43,153 tons, *Ile de France* was not the largest liner in the world, nor the fastest at 23.5 knots. Her exterior was quite similar to that of *Paris*—straight stem, three equally-spaced red and black funnels and a counter stern—though she had her lifeboats on gravity davits giving her greater deck space.

Ile de France nonetheless represented the dawn-ing of a new age. She was the first brand new large liner to be introduced since *Vaterland* in 1914, and the jet-setters of the day were eager to sail in something new. While her exterior was traditional, her interior was not. French Line's president, Jean Piaz, said 'To live is not to copy; it is to create'. With that pronouncement, the top European and French designers were summoned to French Line's headquarters. Gone were the re-creations of castles and chateaux and in their place came what was later known as art deco. Wood veneer was used extensively, along with glass and the French passion for statues, bas-reliefs, enamel panels and paintings by France's leading artists.

First class passengers entered *Ile de France* on A-Deck through her four-deck-high entrance foyer with its towering arches. Two decks up on

Promenade Deck was a parade of magnificent public rooms. The Grand Salon had forty red-columns and contained gilt statues along each side, an Aubusson carpet to cover the dance floor and chairs covered in chintz. Nowhere was a bracket or lampshade to be seen; illumination was indirect and throughout the liner the designers had contrived to hide the lights. Aft of the Salon was a marble-clad grand staircase that swept all the way down to C-Deck. Proceeding aft, passengers entered the Salon de Thé, the rendezvous spot for tea. Last was the smoking-room, combining a cabaret and a 27 ft (8.3 m) bar, the longest afloat. The taproom was built especially for thirsty Americans during Prohibition!

Three decks down was the *salle à manger* designed by Pierre Patout, to which seven hundred diners made the obligatory grand descent via an elaborate staircase into a vast chamber in three shades of grey marble from the Pyrenees, and illuminated by rectangular ceiling lights. In the centre of the room was an over-scale imitation fountain. The chapel, the first such room to

be permanently fitted in a ship, had seats for 80 worshippers and was designed in Gothic style complete with fourteen pillars. Finally, there was the gymnasium that contained bicycles, electric steeds, punching bags and, after the 1933 refit, a full-size boxing ring.

Each of the *Ile de France's* 390 first class cabins was decorated differently. In addition, there was an assortment of lush suites to choose from. Finally, all cabins featured beds instead of bunks. That was the appeal of this new French lady—she was different. Moderately-scaled public rooms, handsome without being grand, comfortable without being overstuffed, class-conscious without living by exclusions, and arriving at a time when Americans, particularly young Americans, were flocking to Europe and wanted a little French 'ooh-la-la' before arriving at Le Havre!

Second class facilities were also of a high standard. The smoking-room was described as 'a very clubby place' with wooden pillars supporting a low ceiling studded with soft lights. Equally cosy were the lounge and dining-room. Rooms and corridors were fully carpeted and

Left *The launching of* Ile de France *on 14 March 1927* (Frank O. Braynard Collection).

Right *The magnificent first class Dining Room of* Ile de France; *note the fountain in the middle of the room* (Frank O. Braynard Collection).

Left Ile de France's *Grand Salon*—*note the columns and statues and not a bracket or lampshade to be seen* (Frank O. Braynard Collection).

Right *Launching a plane from the stern of* Ile de France (National Archives, Washington DC).

Below right Ile de France *after her 1932 refit. The 'air mail' service ended but the catapult is still there. The triple deck Grand Café facing aft resembles a wheelhouse.* (National Archives, Washington DC).

an elevator whisked passengers between the five decks.

Ile de France sailed into New York to a traditional harbour welcome of fire-boats, harbour craft and private yachts. For the next twelve years the '*Rue de la Paix* of the Atlantic' made 347 voyages carrying such celebrities as Arturo Toscanini, Maurice Chevalier, Will Rogers, John D. Rockefeller, Bernard Baruch, Tallulah Bankhead, Gloria Swanson and Barbara Hutton. In fact, she carried more first class passengers in her first eight years of service than any other transatlantic liner.

She kept herself ahead of the rest by being innovative, and in 1928 she managed to capture the limelight again when a plane-launching catapult was installed high on her afterdeck. It was designed and built as a means of shortening mail delivery by a full 24 hours when the ship was one day out of New York or Le Havre. The maiden

flight of this new 'airmail' service occurred on 13 August, when Lieutenant Louis-Marie Demougeot and his radio man climbed into a Loire & Oliver biplane and took off while *Ile de France* was four miles from Sandy Hook. This service, which also became part of the entertainment, continued until 30 October 1930. North German Lloyd's *Bremen* was fitted with a similar device in 1929. *Ile de France* made news again on 1 August 1930 when she sailed from New York with the first miniature golf course installed on a liner. This amusement was a nine-hole course, 40 ft by 80 ft, covered with artificial grass and placed on Sun Deck.

Vibration proved to be a very serious problem with many new ships and *Ile de France* was no exception. French Line partly rectified the situation in a refit that lasted from November 1932 to April 1933. All panelling was removed, padded, and then replaced; there was also a refurbishing

of the public rooms, including extending the Sun Deck to give her the only triple-deck smoking-room, which was renamed the Grand Café. This addition gave the effect of a small bridge facing aft.

She left St Nazaire at 43,450 gross tons and with a revised capacity of 670 first, 408 tourist and 508 third class passengers. Minimum fare one way for the 1933 summer season across the Atlantic from America was $212 (£53) first class. For the frugal who also desired respectability, tourist class was $108.50 (£27) and for the under-paid pedagogue who longed for a summer abroad, a third class ticket was $79 (£20).

At the outbreak of the Second World War, *Ile de France* was at her New York berth. French Line wisely cancelled all future sailings, and, with no place to go, the liner was towed to Staten Island and laid up. The majority of her crew were shipped home, leaving a skeleton staff of 100 to maintain the liner. In March 1940, under the command of the British Admiralty to whom the liner was on loan, *Ile de France* proceeded to Marseilles, then departed shortly afterwards for Cape Town and Saigon. Following the collapse of France in June 1940, *Ile de France* was diverted to Singapore where she was formally seized by the British. She reappeared in New York during the autumn of 1941 and proceeded to Todd Shipyards; her machinery was over-

hauled, her entire plumbing system was scrapped and replaced and she was converted into a troopship with berths for 9,706 servicemen. She was then dispatched back to the Pacific with an Indian crew under P & O management, flying the dual flags of Great Britain and the Free French Naval Forces.

Ile de France was first based at Saigon, then Bombay where she undertook voyages to the Red Sea. Later she was placed on the Cape Town-Suez shuttle in company with Cunard's *Mauretania* and Holland-America's *Nieuw Amsterdam*. In 1943, she was back on the North Atlantic with a European crew under Cunard-White Star management. Finally, she was de-commissioned on 22 September 1945 and handed back to French Line. She was then used for repatriation and austerity voyages to Indo-China, Canada and the US; she departed for the latter from Cherbourg on 22 October 1946, her first post-war commercial sailing. When her duties were finally over, *Ile de France* was re-turned to her builders for a much needed over-haul and refit. For her war service, she was awarded the Croix de Guerre with Palm.

Ile de France emerged with a different profile and style. The public rooms on Promenade Deck

Ile de France *departing on another trooping voyage* (National Archives, Washington DC).

After the war, Ile de France *returned to service sporting two funnels* (Frank O. Braynard Collection).

were altered to meet the changing times. For-ward, in place of the pre-war cabins, was now a drawing-room with its own stairway leading up to a smoking-room and small bar on Boat Deck. The main lounge became a theatre, the Salon de Thé was made into the Grand Salon with an orchestra stand and the Grand Café was now a one-deck-high smoking-room. She was now 44,356 gross tons and her capacity was limited to 541 first class, 577 cabin class and 227 tourist class passengers. Sporting two red, black topped funnels instead of three, *Ile de France* resumed operation on 21 July 1949 from He Havre. A glance at the 1955 fares shows that a first class passage started at £121 ($340), cabin at £113 ($235) and tourist at £64 ($180).

During these twilight years, the most dramatic event in her career was the rescue of 753 people from the stricken Italian liner *Andrea Doria* on 26 July 1956. Three months later she was caught in a violent Atlantic storm which dented her super-structure and flooded six cabins. On 21 February 1957, *Ile de France* departed from New York on an 18-day Caribbean cruise, with rates ranging from $510 (£182) for an inside cabin without facilities to $2,275 (£813) for either the Versailles or Fontainebleau suites. On leaving Fort de France, Martinique, on 26 February, she went aground at Nego Point. She was refloated and returned to Fort de France for a survey which revealed rudder damage; she was then towed by the American salvage vessel *Cable* to Newport News for repairs.

On 26 July 1956, French Line placed an order with Chantiers de l'Atlantique for the building of a 50,000-ton (later 66,000-ton) steamer to be named *France*. At 29 years old, *Ile de France* was still a formidable rival along with her consort *Liberté*, the former *Europa* built in 1930. How-ever, age and high maintenance costs spelled her doom; she departed from New York for the last time on 10 November 1958, and arrived in Le Havre on 17 November.

Declining offers from Sheraton, stating that they would only sell her for scrap, French Line kept *Ile de France* laid up until she was purchased by Yamamoto & Co of Osaka. Renamed Furansu Maru ('French ship') and under the command of a small Japanese crew, she sailed from Le Havre for Osaka on 26 February 1959 watched by saddened admirers. At Osaka, a Shinto altar was erected, there were offerings of food to the gods and a thousand guests attended a ceremony of purification so that *Ile de France* could aproach the gods with her soul immaculate, a fitting end for a magnificent liner that did indeed possess a soul and had achieved a kind of maritime canonization.

Andrew Stone, a Metro Golwyn Mayer producer, approached Yamamoto & Co and asked if he could both lease the ship and assist in the scrapping by using her in a film entitled *The Last Voyage*, about the sinking of a luxury liner. He explained that the ship was going to be scrapped anyway and he would also help in the salvage operations afterwards. The Japanese, having committed the *Furansu Maru's* soul to the gods, saw no problem in this, and therefore leased the ship. French Line interceded and wanted the name *Ile de France* struck from the script; all parties concurred on that point and the ship was renamed *Claridon* for the film. The legendary lady had her bulkheads blown out, her boiler blown up and her forward funnel made to collapse on to the bridge, then she was made to sink bow first. After shooting, she was refloated and scrapped at Osaka, truly an undignified way for a liner with a soul to end.

Normandie

(Lafayette)

Builders Chantiers et Ateliers de St Nazaire (Penhoët), St Nazaire, 1935
Specifications 79,280 gross tons; 1,030 ft (314 m) long, 117 ft (36 m) wide
Machinery Turbo-electric engines; quadruple screw; speed 29 knots
Passengers 848 first class, 670 tourist class, 454 third class
Demise Burned in 1942

CGT's flagship displaying her beautiful lines before the 1935 refit (Author's Collection).

The launching of Normandie *on 29 October 1934* (Everett E. Viez, SSHSA Collection).

If there was ever a 'ship beautiful', that epithet would rightfully belong to the *Normandie*, for she represented the pinnacle of French shipbuilding and design. Not wanting to be left behind by the British, Germans and Italians who were planning or constructing enormous steamers, French Line's engineers went to the drawing-boards and in 1930 placed an order with Chantiers, thus fulfilling three-quarters of its 1912 commitment. The keel of this ship was laid down on 26 January 1931 and was known as 'T6 BIS'. Work progressed despite the Depression and a slowing down of the work in the hope of a future upturn in tourist travel, and on 29 October 1932 Madame LeBrun, wife of the French President, swung a bottle of French champagne and christened 'T6 BIS' *Normandie*. The giant 27,657-ton hull, at the time the heaviest object to move on land, slid down the launchways.

Normandie's completion was not without incident. On a few occasions, work was slowed down when there was Government doubt concerning the feasibility of such lavish expenditure during those harsh economic times. Saboteurs were also at work in January and May 1935. A Penhoët supervisor walking down a *Normandie* alleyway noticed some of the ship's wall panels loose. He unscrewed them for closer inspection and exposed the electrical conduits. He found needles sticking out of the conduits, and, removing other panels, found more needles and some conduits cut. The idea was apparently to short circuit the system and create an electrical fire. Eight days before her maiden departure on 21 May, a watchman on his rounds heard people running from a room near the upper bridge. He went to investigate and saw two men; he shouted but they ignored him, so instead he entered the room they had just left. He discovered a pail of fuel oil ablaze with flames inches from the curtains. He grabbed an extinguisher and put out the fire. Had the watchman not so conscientiously entered the room, there would probably have been no *Normandie*.

Normandie was completed in May 1935. Re-

sponsible for her modern hull design and lines was the Russian emigré Vladimir Yourkevitch, who had given her a rounded stem and a bulbous bow beneath the water. Gone was the clutter on the upper decks. The forward end was protected by a 'whale-back' under which the deck machinery and capstans were cleverly concealed. She had three red and black streamlined funnels that decreased progressively in height, the aftermost being a dummy in whose base were housed the kennels. The foremast was stepped from the bridge and the mainmast from the superstructure abaft the funnels. The after decks were nicely terraced down to the special semi-counter stern. From almost any angle, *Normandie* was pleasing to the eye.

After very successful trials, *Normandie* was formally handed over to CGT on 23 May. A round of parties followed to acquaint France's leading figures in politics, society, the arts and literature with the new Queen of the Oceans. The guests, and later passengers, were enthralled. To provide the naval architects and designers with 'adequate' space in which to work, the engineers had arranged for the engine-room uptakes to be divided. The results represented the epitome of France's decorative art encapsulated in the most ravishing public rooms ever to be seen at sea. French Line had spent 800 million francs on its new belle and it showed.

The first class passengers embarked on C-Deck into an entrance hall that occupied an area of 1,980 sq ft. Facing aft were two 20 ft tall bronze doors that led into one of the most magnificent chambers ever built in a ship, the air-conditioned *salle à manger* designed by Pierre Potout. A flight of stairs enabled diners to make the grand descent into a room at 305 ft slightly longer than the Hall of Mirrors at Versailles; it was 46 ft wide and three decks high. The walls glittered with tiles of moulded glass and vertical strips of hammered glass. In its centre stood a 13 ft toga-clad woman, 'La Paix' by Dejean. Illumination was by 38 vertical glass fixtures mounted on the glass-panelled walls supplemented by 12 glass light fountains lit from within and two decorative glass chandeliers. Aubusson needle-point art deco chairs grouped around 157 covered tables completed the setting of that palatial saloon. On each side of the main dining-room were four ornamental bronze doors that opened on to a like number of smaller private dining-rooms, each 17 ft by 9 ft. For the select few not satisfied with CGT's 'normal' first class cuisine, *Normandie* provided an alternative, the Grill Room aft on Boat Deck overlooking the terraced aft decks and ocean. Between meals the room served as an observation lounge and bar and in the evening, after dinner, a night club. Entering the Grill Room, guests found themselves at the top of a grand staircase that led to *Normandie's* first class public rooms. Near the top stood 'La Normandie', a 7 ft 8 in tall lacquered bronze statue by Baudry. From this vantage point, assuming that all the doors were open, it was possible to see through the smoking-room,

main lounge and all the way to the backdrop at the rear of the stage in the theatre.

Descending the stairway, guests entered the smoking-room panelled in Coromandel lacquer with gilt overlays and carved to depict hunting scenes, fishing and other pastimes. Brown morocco leather chairs were grouped around lacquered card-tables on a carpeted floor. Separating the smoking-room from the main lounge was a lacquer panel that could slide away to join the two rooms. The main lounge was 110 ft long and 85 ft wide and extended for two decks. It was decorated with four etched and painted glass panels and furnished with tapestry-covered floral-design chairs and divans. The windows of the apartment were hung with full-length embroidered silk curtains.

Guests then entered the lounge vestibule and upper entrance hall where the elevators and staircases were located. Forward was the theatre, the first permanent one on a ship, complete with 380 red velvet seats, stage equipment, lighting and dressing-rooms. Its walls and ceilings were silver-coloured and it was illuminated by recessed lighting fixtures. At the extreme forward end of the deck was the Winter Garden, accessible

Above left *Another New York departure* (Author's collection).

Right *The Smoking Room and the grand stairway leading to the Grill Room. The statue at the top of the stairway is 'La Normandie'* (Author's Collection).

Left *The lustrous Salle à Manger with its twelve 'light fountains' and sculpture of 'La Paix' by Dejean* (Author's Collection).

Below Normandie's *Winter Garden with real birds in the cages* (Author's Collection).

Below right *The main lounge of* Normandie (Author's Collection).

from the port and starboard sides of the enclosed Promenade Deck. This room was artistically decorated with flowers, plants, bubbling fountains and two ornamental birdcages that contained tropical birds which serenaded the guests. At the curved front of the room were 28 windows, each designed to withstand the fury of the North Atlantic. Adjoining the after side of the Winter Garden was the writing-room on the port side and the 5,000-book library on the starboard. Other facilities included a two-level chapel that seated 100 worshippers, a complete gymnasium and the largest swimming-pool installed on a ship. It was 75 ft long and 18 ft wide, with the walls, ceiling and surrounding terraces covered by tiles of pale blue enamelled sandstone executed in mosaic and floral patterns.

There were 431 first class cabins decorated in 431 different ways. Her most sumptuous accommodation were the Trouville and the Deauville Suites located at the ship's stern on Sun Deck. Each suite had four bedrooms, a living-room with a grand piano, a dining-room, a pantry, a servant's bedroom, five baths or half-baths and a private promenade 45 ft by 15 ft. For the less ostentatious, there were other de luxe suites from which to choose.

Tourist class public facilities and staterooms were arranged on the aft of the first class. The dining saloon was on C-Deck and was 103 ft wide and 66 ft long. Its central dome extended to the deck above and was supported by five massive glass columns. Three decks higher was the lounge panelled in polished grained sycamore with embellishments of decorative glass and furnished with Aubusson-covered chairs. Adjacent, to its aft, was the library and snack-bar, while aft on Promenade Deck was the semi-circular smoking-room with full-length windows overlooking the promenades aft. The mural treatment was of walnut while the electric lighting was in the form of luminous bands and strips.

Provisions were made for the carriage of an unusually small number of third class passengers. Allocated to the extreme rear of the ship, third

class boasted a lounge panelled in ash and furnished with green morocco leather chairs, a smoking-room decorated with varnished mahogany and furnished with upholstered red leather chairs, and a dining-room which seated 235 passengers. The walls of the apartment were covered by yellow Caramy marble, while the columns supporting the dome were finished in veneered mahogony. The cabins accommodated two, three or four persons, and for the first time tourist and third class each had its own lift.

To guard against fire, non-combustible materials were used extensively. These included fireproof paint, glass and stainless steel. To warn of imminent danger, an elaborate system of fire detection was incorporated, and fire extinguishing equipment was located throughout the liner.

On 29 May 1935, accompanied by a hysterical entourage of hooting watercraft, buzzing aeroplanes and shrieking crowds, Commandant-Adjutant Réné Pugnet eased his ship away from her landing-stage at Le Havre. He pointed *Normandie* north towards Southampton, where she was welcomed with a rendition of the Marseillaise. Three hundred guests disembarked, and when *Normandie* weighed anchor there were 1,013 passengers aboard who had paid from £56 ($270) first class, £29 ($138.50) tourist class and £19 ($93) for the passage to New York. Four days, three hours and two minutes later, at an average speed of 29.98 knots, *Normandie* was in New York. Having arrived prepared, a 50 ft blue pennant was unfurled and run up *Normandie's* mainmast telling all she was the new Blue Riband holder. *Normandie* steamed up the Hudson River to a rapturous welcome by a flotilla of water-craft and over 200,000 people who witnessed her progression from quarantine to her berth at 48th Street. Dignitaries from all over the metropolitan area paid their respects, and four days later, 7 June, *Normandie* departed with 1,600 passengers for England and France. Her average speed during the crossing was 30.31 knots, breaking all existing records. On 19 July she departed Le Havre on a weekend cruise with 1,700 French tourists which ended at Southampton on 21 July.

It became obvious that French Line would have to solve one problem that made its appearance during trials—that of vibration—or suffer negative comments from passengers and adverse publicity from rivals. On her last sailing from New York for the 1935 season, the Duke of Sutherland presented *Normandie* with the Hales Trophy, and when she arrived at Le Havre in October, she was withdrawn from service and sent to St Nazaire. The work that was carried out included cutting an expansion joint in the superstructure just aft of the Grill Room, removing six of the light fountains in the dining-room, installing friction stanchions throughout the ship, tearing out the double-deck tourist class salon and redividing the space into two decks, thus stiffening each deck. In that operation 20 new tourist class cabins were added and to replace the missing lounge a new one was built on Boat Deck, just aft of the Grill Room, eliminating the latter's view. The cabins and new lounge increased her tonnage from 79,280 to 83,423 gross tons, assuring her place as the largest ship in the world, a distinction she kept until the arrival in 1940 of *Queen Elizabeth*. Other alterations and additions were to reinforce the shaft bossings, add 80 tons of steel to her stern, add 200 tons of pig iron to the ship's forward ballast tanks to keep her in trim and fit her with new four-bladed propellers. The most notable addition was the installation of a radar device for detecting objects in a ship's path, and *Normandie* was the first passenger liner to have one.

After three trials in April, the practically vibration-free *Normandie* was ready to resume the North Atlantic run. During an underwater inspection the day before sailing, the divers reported that all three propellors were there; *Normandie's* engineers found this odd since she was a quadruple screw ship! Another inspection confirmed the divers' report, so she was hurried into dry dock, had two of her three-bladed propellers replaced on her inboard tail shafts and was dispatched to New York on 6 May 1936. *Normandie* vibrated her way across the Atlantic and back, and upon her return to Le Havre, new four-bladed propellers were cast and fitted to the liner. French Line was saved.

In 1936, *Normandie* suffered two indignities. The first was the loss of the Blue Riband to

Normandie *after her 1935 refit sporting her new tourist class lounge on Boat Deck* (W. B. Taylor, SSHSA Collection).

Queen Mary, and the second was the downgrading of her first class accommodation to cabin class in order to compete with the 'Queen' which was designated a 'cabin class' ship. In March 1937, however, *Normandie* regained the Blue Riband by steaming from Ambrose to Bishop Rock in 4 days 6 minutes at an average speed of 30.99 knots. She improved on this in August, covering the distance in 3 days 22 hours 7 minutes, and in July she had captured the westbound Blue Riband by steaming from Bishop Rock to Ambrose in 3 days 23 hours 2 minutes at an average speed of 30.58 knots, becoming the first ship to cover the 2,906 miles westbound in under four days. *Queen Mary*, however, proved to be the faster of the giants, and she settled the speed question in August 1938 by achieving an average speed of 30.99 knots westbound and 31.69 knots eastbound.

On 5 February 1938, *Normandie* departed from New York on a 22-day South American cruise under the auspices of Raymond-Whitcomb Travel. Ports of call were Nassau, Trinidad, Rio de Janeiro and Martinique with prices ranging from $790 (£158) to $9,970 (£1,990) for one of the de luxe suites on Boat Deck. She became the largest and fastest ship ever to cross the equator. The South American cruise was repeated again on 4 February 1939, when her 1,000 passengers visited Nassau, Trinidad, Rio, Barbados and Martinique before returning to New York on 28 February.

In April 1939 French Line entertained the idea of building a consort to *Normandie*. Drawings had been made and the vessel had been tentatively named *Bretagne* when the Second World War intervened and France fell in June 1940. The *Bretagne* project was cancelled.

Normandie sailed on 16 August 1939 on what proved to be her last departure from New York, and arrived back in America on 28 August with 1,417 nervous passengers. Three days later, war broke out in Europe and French Line cancelled the rest of *Normandie's* sailings. She had made 139 North Atlantic crossings and had carried 133,170 passengers, an average of 958 per crossing, not an impressive figure. It was often stated that the immense proportions of her lounges and the glamour of their decor overwhelmed many, making them feel like mice in a cathedral. She did, however, appeal to certain groups—the nouveaux riches, the artists and the left-of-centre crowd who kept late hours. Among the many personalities who graced her were Josephine Baker, Irving Berlin, Pierre Cartier, Walter P. Chrysler, Noel Coward, Marlene Dietrich, Max Factor, Douglas Fairbanks Jr, Herbert Hoover, Cole Porter, Mrs Paul Robeson, Edward G. Robinson, Arturo Toscanini, Igor Stravinsky and Gloria Vanderbilt, to name but a few. Despite her opulent interiors and her passenger lists, *Normandie* was a money loser. In fact, she was not built to make profits, but to serve as a floating symbol of the Third Republic. In that capacity she had succeeded admirably.

Most of *Normandie*'s crew were taken home in other French Line vessels and a skeleton crew remained to care for the liner. On 12 December 1941, *Normandie* was seized by the United States and handed over to the United States Navy to be converted into the troop transport *Lafayette,* AP 53. During the process of conversion, disaster struck. As a safety measure to prevent injury to troops, the Navy had the four stanchions in the Grand Salon removed; these were the ones

added in 1936 to solve the vibration problem. On 9 February 1942, at about 2.30 pm, Clement Derrick was in the process of removing one of these stanchions. During the process, sparks from his acetylene torch flew on to the burlap covering the life-preservers stuffed with kapok. Within seconds the bale was afire. There was no fire watch, no observation by the foreman on the

Normandie burning at her New York berth on 9 February 1942 (National Archives, Washington DC).

Salvage begins with the removal of the superstructure of Normandie. Note the cranes by the bridge and the aft funnel (National Archives, Washington DC).

job, no hose ready and no fire extinguishers. The men tried to put out the growing flames, but the choking black smoke drove them from the salon. The fire department was called and both land and maritime units arrived. Water was poured into the burning liner and she started to take on a list; by 2.20 am *Lafayette* had rolled over on her side, her three funnels parallel to the ice-clogged water of the slip.

Work to salvage *Lafayette* started at the end of February with the removal of the third dummy funnel, and by 8 August 1943, *Lafayette* was afloat though listing at 49°. On 27 October 1943,

she was upright in her dock, minus her super-structure. Seven days later, 3 November, twenty tugs towed her from her pier to the Navy Yard at Bayonne, New Jersey. Plans were advanced to either convert her into a troop-ship or an auxiliary aircraft carrier, and in preparation for this the hull was towed to Todd Shipyard in Broklyn on 11 January 1944. However, with the war in the Allies' favour and now drawing to a close, both plans were cancelled. The Navy declared her surplus property and subsequently sold her to Julius Lipsett for $161,680. On 28 November 1946, what was once the pride of the French merchant marine commenced her final voyage under the tow of twelve tugs to Newark, New Jersey, where she was scrapped. It was an inglorious end to one of the most beautiful flagships ever to sail the oceans.

Left *The once mighty Normandie, now a hull on her side* (National Archives, Washington DC).

Right *Towed by 20 tugs, the Normandie's chalked hull makes its last voyage down the Hudson River* (National Archives, Washington DC).

Right *The last remains of what many considered to be the most beautiful ship in the world* (National Archives, Washington DC).

Cunard-White Star Line

Queen Mary

Builders John Brown & Company Ltd,
Clydebank, 1936
Specifications 80,774 gross tons; 1,019 ft
(310 m) long, 118 ft (36 m) wide
Machinery Parsons geared turbines; quadruple
screw; speed 29 knots
Passengers 776 cabin class, 784 tourist class, 579
third class
Demise Hotel and museum at Long Beach,
California

In 1926, Cunard executives began serious deliberations on replacing their older express tonnage. Concurrently, Cunard's rivals were busily planning or constructing superliners—*Bremen*, *Europa*, *Rex*, *Conti de Savoia*, *Normandie* and *Oceanic*. Therefore, in order to remain competitive, Cunard announced in May 1930 that an order had been placed at Clydebank for a giant liner known as 'No 534'. The keel of this mammoth ship was laid on 27 December 1930 and for a year building proceeded apace.

The Depression took its toll on Atlantic shipping and Cunard, facing financial constraints, suspended construction on 'No 534'. Cunard losses for 1931 were £533,204, and they could not possibly build this leviathan without govern-

ment assistance. Trimming their fleet to show fiscal responsibility, Cunard approached the British Government for a loan. After lengthy presentations, the Government granted Cunard's request. It was prepared to advance £3 million to complete the ship, £1.5 million as working capital and a further £5 million if Cunard decided to build a sister ship. The only string attached to this deal was that Cunard and White Star Line merge. In a formal agreement signed in February 1934, the assets of the two companies were amalgamated into Cunard-White Star Limited, and White Star cancelled construction of its *Oceanic*.

With the infusion of capital, work resumed on 'No 534' on 3 April 1934. Five months later, she was ready to be launched. Amid much jingoism, on a grey and rainy Wednesday afternoon on 16 September 1934, the Royal Family, executives from Cunard-White Star and John Brown and thousands of onlookers witnessed the momentous occasion. At ten minutes past three, Her Majesty Queen Mary snipped the satin cord holding a bottle of Australian white wine, sending it crashing against the bow plates. As the bottle shattered, she pressed a small button to fire the launch triggers, and speaking in public for the first time said 'I am happy to name this ship *Queen Mary* . . . I wish success to her and to all who sail in her'. Slowly, 35,600 tons of metal—the heaviest object yet to move on land—inched then thundered its way into the River Clyde.

Queen Mary was towed to the fitting-out basin and completed on 15 April 1936. After a series of

Left *The heaviest object to move on land—the launching of* Queen Mary *on 16 September 1934* (Frank O. Braynard Collection).

The maiden arrival of Queen Mary *in New York, 1 June 1936 (Frank O. Braynard Collection).*

successful trials, she was handed over to Cunard on 12 May to become its flagship, and Britain's largest merchant ship. Her coming-out party took place at Southampton, and was attended by Their Majesties the King and Queen and their royal party, dignitaries, wealthy celebrities and the press.

The day of judgement arrived on 27 May 1936, when *Queen Mary*, loaded with 1,742 passengers and a crew of 1,101, departed from Southampton on her maiden voyage to New York under the command of Captain Sir Edgar T. Britten. After a brief call at Cherbourg where 107 more passengers embarked, her four screws, the world's largest at 35 tons each, propelled her across the Atlantic at an average speed of 29.13 knots. *Queen Mary* arrived at New York on 1 June 1936, and steamed majestically up the Hud-

son River to a tumultuous welcome. Passage fares for the inaugural season started at £57 ($282) cabin, £30 ($149) tourist and £19 ($93) third class.

In August 1936, *Queen Mary* captured the westbound record by steaming between Bishop Rock and Ambrose in 4 days 27 minutes at an average speed of 30.14 knots. The return east-bound voyage was made in 3 days 23 hours 57 minutes at an average speed of 30.63 knots, gaining the coveted Blue Riband from *Normandie* and becoming the first ship to cross the Atlantic in under four days. In March, July and August 1937, *Normandie* improved her speed and won back the trophy for both the east and west crossings, but in 1938 *Queen Mary* finally settled the battle of the Riband. On 4 August, she left Southampton, called at Cherbourg, then, reaching an average speed of 30.99 knots, arrived at Ambrose 3 days 21 hours 48 minutes later on 8 August. On her return voyage, *Queen Mary* steamed from Ambrose to Bishop Rock in 3 days 20 hours 42 minutes at an average speed of 31.69 knots. That record remained unchallenged until the commissioning of *United States* in 1952.

While *Queen Mary's* competitors introduced innovative technical and interior design to the high seas, Cunard opted for the traditional look in the style of a comfortable English manor. The exterior of the Queen Mary resembled a streamlined version of the *Berengaria* of 1913 vintage, and her interior designers working with 56 different woods strove for 'restrained modernism with a result of subdued elegance'—a scaled down version of *Aquitania's* interior of 1914.

What *Queen Mary's* public rooms lacked in flamboyance was made up for in their dimensions. On C-Deck was the largest apartment ever built within a ship, the cabin class restaurant entered through silver-metal glazed screens. The

Outbound is Queen Mary, *while arriving at New York is Italian Line's* Giulio Cesare *(Frank O. Braynard Collection).*

chamber was 143 ft long and 118 ft wide and was surmounted by a large dome extending two decks. Based on the theme of 'warm, restful shades of autumn', the room was panelled in three tones of Brazilian peroba. The structural columns were also of peroba interlaced with silver-bronze metal reeds. Seating capacity was provided for 815 diners in sycamore chairs upholstered in autumn red. An interesting decorative feature was a map representing the North Atlantic at the forward upper boundary of the room. During the crossing, an illuminated model in crystal indicated the position of the ship on its voyage between Europe and the United States. Also on C-Deck was the balcony entrance to the cabin class swimming-pool, encompassing an area of 2,520 sq ft.

Social activity was centred on Promenade Deck. At the forward end was the Observation Lounge then aft to starboard was the drawing-room and to port a library. Through the Main Hall and Shopping Centre passengers entered the Main Lounge, a salon 96 ft long and 70 ft wide with a height of three decks, and decorated in golden autumnal tints produced by a combination of maple burr and makore. Aft was the Starboard Gallery and on the other side the Long Gallery, from which the Ballroom was entered, a rather small chamber (35 ft long and 50 ft wide)

The largest chamber ever built in a ship was Queen Mary's *first class Dining Room (Frank O. Braynard Collection).*

with oak flooring and makore veneers. The last public room was the Smoking-Room, panelled in walnut burr and brown oak and furnished with leather chairs. An electric fire added a masculine yet cosy touch. Aft on Sun Deck, for the discriminating gourmet, was the supplementary Verandah Grill. For the physically

active a squash racket court and gymnasium were located on Sports Deck, and four circuits round Sun Deck equalled a mile.

Tourist class public rooms and accommodation were situated in the aft sections of the liner. There was a two-deck high smoking-room on Promenade Deck, a lounge with a dome and a cocktail bar on Main Deck and a smaller lounge on A-Deck. The dining room was on C-Deck and done in ash burr with the upper part in silver-grey blistered maple. For the first time, tourist class enjoyed the use of their own indoor swimming-pool with a gymnasium adjacent. Over eighty per cent of the cabins had a private shower and toilet, and passengers could ride three lifts to reach any of their eight decks. As the 1936 brochure stated, 'Every modern convenience especially designed for the comfort, convenience and pleasure of travellers in this modern age' was available in 'the outstanding marine masterpiece of the day'.

Third class was allocated the forward part of the 'Queen'. Spread out over six decks and accessible by a lift were a Garden Lounge panelled in sycamore, a smoking-room finished in oak veneer, a lounge that served as a library, a cinema panelled in cherrywood and a dining-room decorated in grained sycamore with a dado of coral-coloured mahogany. Cabins were sparsely decorated and possessed no individual facilities.

When the excitement of her inaugural season died down, her critics and some passengers voiced their main concerns about he 'Queen'. All fast liners had vibration problems, and *Queen Mary* was no exception, and this plagued her entire career. Another problem was encountered with the exhaust from her mammoth stacks which Cunard partly remedied, though not until having paid a few ladies' laundry or replacement bills! Finally, she rolled, staying at an angle for an alarming length of time. Because of her size, John Brown had exhibited optimism and neglected to provide handrails along the passageways or anchoring devices for most of the furniture. In 1936, during a severe October storm, it became abundantly clear that even ships of her size were subject to terrifying motion, and Cunard quickly installed handrails and anchored the furniture. However, it was not until 1958 that the rolling problem was corrected.

Yet, despite these minor flaws, *Queen Mary* quickly became a legend on the North Atlantic, enjoying the patronage of the rich and famous. Among the luminaries who voyaged on her were Fred Astaire, Lionel Barrymore, Marlene Dietrich, Clark Gable, Greta Garbo, Oliver Hardy, Bob Hope, Stan Laurel, Jesse Owens, Paul Robeson, the Baron and Baroness de Rothschild, Gloria Swanson and the Duke and Duchess of Windsor. Cunard, reflecting the social mores of the time, did not allow black passengers to travel first or cabin class (whichever was the highest).

The 'Queen' was not only the fastest liner in the world, she was also the second largest, bringing in her share of dividends to Cunard's coffers. Of all the superliners built between 1929 and 1936, only *Queen Mary* made a profit.

Queen Mary departed from Southampton on 30 August 1939 with 2,332 passengers, and when she docked at Pier 90 in New York on 4 September, Britain and Germany were officially at war. Next door at Pier 88 was her rival, *Normandie*. Most of *Queen Mary's* crew was sent home, leaving a skeleton staff behind to keep her tidy. In March 1940, she was joined at Pier 90 by her future running-mate *Queen Elizabeth*, the largest liner ever built. In the same month, Cunard learned that its beloved ship was needed for military duty. Painted battleship grey and her name obliterated, *Queen Mary* departed on 21 March for Sydney, Australia, where she arrived on 17 April. Her passenger fittings were removed and her interior converted into a troopship capable of transporting 5,500 soldiers. Anti-aircraft machine-guns were mounted at strategic locations on the upper decks and a six-inch gun was anchored to her stern. To protect her from magnetic mines, an electronic degaussing strip was attached to the ship's hull to repel underwater explosives.

Eighteen days later, the stupendous task of conversion was completed and the 'Queen' was ordered to embark 5,000 Australian troops for England. She left on 5 May 1940 in the 'multi-million dollar' convoy 'US3' that included six other luxury liners. At Cape Town, the convoy split up and *Queen Mary* continued on to Gourock, arriving on 16 June. She left the Clyde on 29 June for Singapore, and after an overhaul proceeded in September down to Sydney, where she embarked troops and departed for Bombay in October 1940. Another overhaul and dry-docking was ordered in February 1941 at Singapore, after which she returned to Sydney and left in March on a round trip to Fremantle. *Queen Mary* and *Queen Elizabeth* met outside Sydney harbour for the first time in April 1941 and, along with *Mauretania*, set out for Suez on 9 April. *Queen Mary* undertook three more round voyages to Suez in 1941, then, on 19 December,

The 'Grey Ghost' at speed (National Archives, Washington DC).

she headed north via Trincomalee (Ceylon) and Cape Town to arrive in New York on 12 January 1942, and shortly thereafter in Boston for additional armament and 'berths'. 20 mm guns were mounted on the upper decks, six three-inch guns augmented the six-inch gun on the stern and near the after funnel and four sets of anti-aircraft rocket launchers were installed. Standee bunks were erected in the lounges, drawing-rooms and even the swimming-pools.

Queen Mary headed south again on 18 February 1942 with 8,398 troops sailing via Key West, Rio de Janeiro and Cape Town for Sydney, arriving on 28 March. Departing on 6 April, she sailed back to New York with a crew of 832 and 58 passengers. On 11 May, the 'Queen' launched the 'GI Shuttle'—ferrying troops, the wounded, prisoners of war and dignitaries like Winston Churchill between England and the United States—when she set out for Gourock with 9,880 American troops and a crew of 875. Her total capacity was 10,755, and this was the first time that more than 10,000 people had sailed in a ship. Later in the month she was detoured to Suez, leaving that port on 23 June for New York, whereupon she resumed the 'GI Shuttle' service.

On 27 September, *Queen Mary* sailed from New York with 10,398 troops. Five days out, on 2 October, disaster occurred. The 'Queen' and HMS *Curacoa*, a cruiser assigned to guard the

liner, were both cruising at full speed. Responding to a suspected U-boat, *Queen Mary* wheeled to starboard. Meanwhile, *Curacoa*, also answering the submarine alert, veered to port. The cruiser cut in front of the oncoming *Queen Mary's* specially strengthened bow and was sliced in half. Because Admiralty orders forbade the 'Queen' to stop, to avoid the possibility of presenting a perfect target, the only thing those on board could do was to toss lifebelts and life-preservers overboard. All told, 338 sailors of *Curacoa* perished. *Queen Mary* proceeded to England at a reduce speed of 15 knots, and emergency repairs were made on the dented bow at Gourock, with full repairs being made in Boston. She resumed service as a troop-ship on 8 December 1942 when she departed with over 10,000 troops for Gourock.

Two days before Christmas, the 'Queen' was again detoured to Suez with 10,896 troops. There she embarked 9,995 soldiers and, in convoy with *Aquitania*, *Nieuw Amsterdam* and *Queen of Bermuda*, departed from Suez on 25 January 1943 for Sydney. Her last sailing from 'down under' was in March 1943, to Gourock via Cape Town and Freetown with 8,326 passengers, including 4,050 Italian prisoners taken from South Africa to England. In May 1943, *Queen Mary* was permanently placed, along with *Queen Elizabeth*, on the 'GI Shuttle' run. *Queen Mary's* greatest day came on 25 July 1943, when she left New York for Gourock with 16,683 persons on board, the highest figure ever carried in a ship. Maintaining top speed, constantly zigzagging and following highly secret courses taking her as far north as Iceland or south as far as the Azores were the keys to *Queen Mary's* success. Hitler reportedly offered the contemporary equivalent of about £58,000 and the Iron Cross with Oak Leaves to any U-boat commander who could sink her.

The war ended in 1945, but *Queen Mary* continued the Herculean task of returning war-weary American and Canadian soldiers and families home. The 'Grey Ghost' was finally relieved of her military duty on 29 September 1946. During the course of hostilities she had carried 810,730 wartime passengers and sailed over 500,000 miles. Returned to Cunard, the 'Queen' spent the next year at Southampton undergoing extensive overhauling and refurnishing. When work was completed, her new tonnage was 81,237 gross tons and her revised capacity was 711 first, 707 cabin and 577 tourist class passengers. *Queen Mary* departed from Southampton on her first post-war voyage to New York on 31 July 1947 with 1,957 passengers. Minimum passage

Imagine if all sailings were this full! Queen Mary's *first arrival in New York after VE Day* (National Archives, Washington DC).

84 Flagships of the Line

rates in 1948 were £90 ($365) first class, £55 ($225) cabin class and £40 ($165) tourist class.

With her running-mate *Queen Elizabeth*, the two liners became the darlings of the travelling public, offering a weekly departure from either New York or Europe. *Queen Mary* was booked up months in advance with such notables as the new Queen herself, Winston Churchill, Anthony Eden, General Dwight Eisenhower, Bob Hope, Liberace, Johnny Mathis, Elizabeth Taylor, Spencer Tracy and Loretta Young. To give them a smoother ride, twin Denny-Brown stabilizers were fitted into *Queen Mary's* tight engine spaces in 1958. Carpeting was also laid down to protect the linoleum from those high pointed heels that became the fashion.

In October of that year, the first jet crossed the Atlantic to England and three years later Cunard was losing money. To help remedy the deficits, Cunard sent *Queen Mary* on a cruise in December 1963, Cunard's first run from England since 1939. That too was a losing proposition as the grand old liner, now too grand and too old, continued to pile up losses to the tune of £750,000 in 1966.

While both *Queen Mary* and *Queen Elizabeth* were at sea on 8 May 1967, Cunard ordered both captains to open a sealed envelope. This act was performed simultaneously by both and the message stated that *Queen Mary* would be retired in the autumn and *Queen Elizabeth* a year later.

Suitors to save *Queen Mary* appeared everywhere. Among the many interested parties were an octogenarian lady from New England who offered the princely sum of $100 and an elderly gentleman who offered $8 million (imagine Cunard's initial delight until they read further and saw that he wanted to repay the principal at a rate of $100 a year interest free – quick division meant it would have taken him 80,000 years to pay for the ship!). Dr Billy Graham envisaged a floating temple of evangelism, former New York City mayor John Lindsay proposed to use the 'Queen' as a permanently-moored floating crèche for under-privileged children and there was a host of hotel interests. The most serious suitor was the city of Long Beach, and her delegation, led by Vice Mayor Robert F. Crow, flew to London with money in hand to submit their bid. On 24 July, they bid $3,450,000 for the ship and two days later Cunard accepted it. The plan was to convert the 'Queen' into a hotel, convention centre and maritime museum.

The last voyage of *Queen Mary* departed from Southampton on 16 September, arriving at New York on 21 September. The next day, at 11.30 am *Queen Mary* departed from New York on her 1,001st Atlantic crossing, her last, with 1,200 passengers aboard. The New York send-off befitted a Queen. In 31 years of service, *Queen Mary* had steamed more than 3,795,000 miles and carried 2,115,000 fare-paying passengers. Arriving in Southampton, a two-week cruise followed to Las Palmas.

In an attempt to defray some of the delivery cost, the Long Beach delegation requested that the voyage west be opened to fare-paying passengers. Cunard reluctantly agreed to provide the manpower and provisions, but declined to book the cruise. Therefore 'The Last Great Cruise' was handled by Diners Club and Fugazy Travel. On Tuesday 31 October 1967, under the command of Captain John Treasure Jones, *Queen Mary*, with 1,040 passengers aboard, was given a rousing yet sombre send off from Southampton. After steaming 14,559 miles and circumnavigating Cape Horn, *Queen Mary*, the last three-stacker in service, arrived at Long Beach on 9 December to a flotilla of welcoming watercraft reminiscent of 1936. At 12.07 pm, Captain Jones positioned the engine telegraph to 'finished with engines', ending the sailing career of one of the most illustrious ships to ever sail the oceans.

Two days after arrival, Captain Jones formally handed over *Queen Mary* to the city of Long Beach. She was struck from the British Registry of Ships, and with her propellers disconnected from the engines, she was technically classed as a 'building'. She was thoroughly gutted and received a facelift costing $72 million. The Hotel Queen Mary opened in May 1971, but profits failed to materialize, forcing Long Beach in 1980 to arrange for Wrather Corporation to take over the management. The latter invested a further $10 million in the 'Hotel' along with the development of the surrounding area and the acquisition of Howard Hughes' flying machine, the Spruce Goose, to help attract visitors.

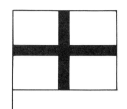

Cyprien Fabre & Compagnie

Patria

Builders Forges & Chantiers de la Méditerranée, La Seyne, 1914
Specifications 11,885 gross tons; 512 ft (156 m) long, 59 ft (18 m) wide
Machinery Triple expansion engines; twin screw; speed 17 knots
Passengers 140 first class, 250 second class, 1,850 third class
Demise Sunk by sabotage in 1940

Fabre Line started operations in the Mediterranean in 1865 and branched out across the Atlantic on a regular basis in 1882. Business prospered culminating in its most successful year, 1913. In 45 voyages, Fabre landed 1,037 first class, 3,214 second and 36,786 steerage class passengers in New York. An additional 231 first class, 744 second class and 12,422 steerage passengers dis-

Patria, *Fabre's flagship from 1914 to 1920* (Henry W. Uhle, SSHSA Collection).

Patria under construction (J. S. Valentine, SSHSA Collection).

embarked in Providence, Rhode Island, on the 26 occasions when a call was made there. The combined eastbound figures from Providence and New York were 1,416 first class, 2,156 second class and 14,962 steerage passengers. It was therefore not surprising that company officials looked forward to the arrival of *Patria* and *Providence* in 1914 and 1915.

Launched on 11 November 1913, *Patria* was completed in less than a year and dispatched across the Atlantic from Marseilles on 16 April 1914. The two-mast, three-funnel (the third was a dummy) liner called at Naples, Palermo and Marseilles, and remained on the North Atlantic during most of the First World War; in later years, additional ports were added to make the crossing more of a cruise.

Patria and her sister *Providence* each had six decks. The top three, A-Deck, B-Deck and C-Deck, were devoted to first class public rooms and cabins. The former consisted of a writing-room, a glass-enclosed verandah, a drawing-room and a smoking-room, 'all carried out with faultless taste, with the object of conveying to their passengers the fullest impression of home comfort during their stay on board'. In addition to all of these public rooms, *Patria* was the first liner to have a cinema installed on board. On D-Deck were the first and second class dining-saloons and the second class smoking-room and drawing-room. Down below on E-Deck and F-Deck were second and third class cabins, third class dormitories and the third class dining-saloon.

The Depression took its toll on transatlantic companies, and cruise-like voyages were not enough to fill Fabre's coffers, so the company had no choice but to withdraw *Patria* from service in 1931. She undertook her last sailing from New York on 20 May 1931, and when she arrived at Marseilles she was laid up pending disposal. The French firm of Messageries Maritimes chartered the liner in January 1932 and eight years later they purchased her; after a quick overhaul, she was placed on the local Marseilles-

Eastern Mediterranean service. Minimum one-way fares in July 1936 from Marseilles to Alexandra, a three-day voyage, were £21 ($106) first class, £15 ($74.80) second class and £11 ($52.80) third class. To Beirut, a six-day trip, they were £28 ($138.60) first class, £20 ($99) second class and £15 ($74.80) third class.

Following France's capitulation, *Patria* was laid up at Haifa. She entered service again in November 1940 under British control. On the 23rd, she was scheduled to leave Haifa for Mauritius with 1,900 emigrants from Palestine, but the sailing date was postponed and the liner remained at Haifa. On 25 November, three explosions rocked the ship. She heeled over and lay on her starboard side on the bottom in shallow water. Two hundred and seventy-nine people fell victim to the act of sabotage, the perpetrators of which were never found. In 1952 the wreck was salvaged and scrapped.

Providence

Builders Forges & Chantiers de la Méditerranée, La Seyne, 1920
Specifications 11,996 gross tons; 512 ft (156 m) long, 59 ft (18 m) wide
Machinery Triple expansion engines; twin screw; speed 17 knots
Passengers 140 first class, 250 second class, 1,850 third class
Demise Scrapped in 1951

Named after the city of Providence, Rhode Island, at which a call was instituted in 1911 by Fabre Line, *Providence* was launched on 14 August 1914. The uncompleted liner was then laid up due to the onset of the First World War, and was not completed until May 1920. Fabre's flagship, and the largest ship the Line ever built, commenced her maiden crossing from Marseilles on 2 June 1920, calling at Lisbon, the Azores, Providence and New York.

Business in 1920 turned out to be even more prolific than the Line's previous most successful year, 1913. In 37 voyages, Fabre carried 58,253 passengers westbound and 32,709 passengers eastbound. Despite fewer voyages than in the earlier year, the increase could in no doubt only be due to its new twin giants, *Patria* and *Providence*. Unfortunately, US immigration laws were changing, and within years the Company was seeking other ways to increase profits.

Like *Patria*, *Providence's* interiors were designed to remind the passengers of the comforts of home. Among those comforts was a large number of outside first-class cabins receiving ventilation and light directly from the promenade decks. Another comfort was French cuisine, concerning which a Fabre brochure claimed 'excellent French cooking, meat breakfast, copious and choice menus, and free table

Providence served on the New York-Mediterranean route (SSHSA Collection).

Providence *in Messageries Maritimes funnel colours* (Compagnie Générale Maritime).

wine'. The above amenities were enjoyed by first class passengers during their Mediterranean cruise lasting 33–35 days in the winter of 1925, costing a minimum of £95 ($450) on a voyage from New York that called at the Azores, Madeira, Algiers, Marseilles, Palermo, Naples, Piraeus, Constantinople, Beirut, Jaffa, Alexandria, Messina and Monaco. The fares included shore excursions and hotels for three days in Egypt. Minimum transatlantic fares from New York to Marseilles, a 15-day voyage in July 1926, were £50 ($245) first class, £28 ($132.50) second class and £18 ($85) third class.

The harsh economic climate forced Fabre to curtail its North Atlantic services. *Providence* departed New York for the last time on 1 February 1931; she was then laid up until char-tered by Messageries Maritimes in January 1932 and placed on its Marseilles-Eastern Mediterranean service. Space was provided for 168 first class, 216 second class, 316 third class and 88 'quatrimes'. *Providence*, along with her sister *Patria*, was sold to Messageries Maritimes in January 1940, and both continued in Mediterranean service.

Following the capitulation of France in June 1940, *Providence* was laid up at Berre near Marseilles. During a storm, her anchor chains broke and the liner was driven ashore. The Government salvaged her on 15 December 1944 and handed her back to Messageries Maritimes who rebuilt her to accommodate 222 first class, 292 second class and 284 third class passengers. She resumed Messageries Maritimes' Mediterranean service after the war, and continued to sail until 1951. In December, *Providence* was sold and taken to La Spezia to be broken up.

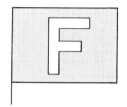

Furness, Withy & Company

Monarch of Bermuda

(New Australia, Arkadia)

Builders Vickers-Armstrong Ltd, Newcastle, 1931
Specifications 22,424 gross tons; 579 ft (177 m) long, 76 ft (23 m) wide
Machinery Steam turbo-electric; quadruple screw; speed 19.5 knots
Passengers 830 first class, 31 second class
Demise Scrapped in 1966

From a distance, Monarch of Bermuda *could easily be mistaken for* Queen Mary *(Author's Collection).*

Furness, Withy & Company, realizing the tourist potential of Bermuda, commissioned three ships in 1919 for the New York-Hamilton run. Proving to be highly popular, Furness sensed the need for more first class tonnage to capture the wealthy American traveller, so in 1928 introduced *Bermuda*. Contemplating a further expansion of first class service during the peak season, Furness laid down *Monarch of Bermuda* in 1930. Launched on 17 March 1931, she was completed in November and commenced her maiden voyage from New York to Hamilton on the 28th of that month.

Powered by a fairly new system, turbo-electric propulsion, the three-funnel (the aftermost being a dummy), two-mast, grey-hulled liner was able to make the voyage in 36 hours. Instead of

Monarch of Bermuda *at Front Street, Hamilton (SSHSA Collection).*

creating 'period' rooms, the designers opted for tasteful, pleasing and cheerful rooms using materials and workmanship of the highest quality. During the crossing and at Bermuda passengers could socialize in the Virgilian Room or the Brummel Lounge, chat in the Galleries (the Brummel's balcony), puff away in the Raleigh Smoke Room, quench their thirsts at The Lotus Verandah Cafe, dine in the full-width dining-saloon, and finally conclude the evening by watching the latest film in the cinema room or dance away the night in the covered 100 ft by 80 ft Dance Hall. There was extensive deck space for outdoor activities and two swimming-pools—one indoors for bathing during the first day out of New York during winter and one outside deck pool. Every first class cabin had a private toilet and full bath or shower, quite a novelty in the 'thirties. Passengers were kept comfortable during hot weather by a Thermo Tank system, a forerunner of today's air conditioning.

Monarch of Bermuda sailed on the 'millionaires' run', with her consort *Queen of Bermuda* introduced in 1933, with litle variation. She was in attendance on 8 September 1934, despite heavy seas and torrential rain, to rescue 71 survivors from the burning *Morro Castle*.

In November 1939, *Monarch of Bermuda* was requisitioned and converted into a troop transport at Liverpool. Carrying as many as 4,000 soldiers at a time, she made voyages to the Middle East, was present during the evacuation of Norway in June 1940 and also participated in 'Operation Torch', the invasion of North Africa and later Italy. She also made her share of transatlantic trooping voyages, and also journeyed to Japan after that nation's collapse to bring home the troops. From a distance, the Germans often mistook her silhouette for that of *Queen Mary*.

After steaming 400,000 miles and carrying 160,000 troops and passengers, *Monarch of Bermuda* was returned to her builders in early 1947 for reconversion into a luxury liner. On 24 March 1947, while at dry dock, a fire swept through the ship, gutting the superstructure and accommodation. She was examined by the Ministry of Transport, which bought the wreck and had it rebuilt into a migrant ship by Thorny-

Above Monarch of Bermuda *in war grey* (Furness, Withy & Company).

Below *The emigrant liner,* New Australia (Furness, Withy & Company).

croft at Southampton. Conversion was completed in 1949 and the liner emerged as the 20,256 gross ton *New Australia*, with accommodation for 1,593 passengers in a single class. Gone were the first and third funnels, and in place of the first funnel was a mast that acted as an engine exhaust. Eliminated also was the mainmast and the enclosed promenade, now open for the southern waters of Australia.

Placed under the managent of the Shaw, Savill & Albion Company, *New Australia* departed from Southampton for Sydney on 15 August 1950. Her route was via the Suez Canal and included calls at Fremantle and Melbourne. In 1953, she was diverted to trooping work in connection with the Korean conflict. Then, with Italian-financed emigrant fleets on the rise, the Ministry of Transport ended its own services to the antipodes and in January 1958 *New Australia* was sold to Greek Line. Renamed *Arkadia*, she was taken into Blohm & Voss for refitting and modernization.

Arkadia emerged as a more streamlined emigrant carrier. A 10 ft section was added to her bow, giving a new length of 589 ft (180 m). Her tonnage was increased to 20,259 (making her Greek Line's new flagship, since *Olympia* was registered in 1955 at 17,362 gross tons) and her passenger accommodation was modified to 150 first class and 1,150 tourist class. Registered under the Arcadia Steamship Company, *Arkadia* left Bremen on her first voyage to Montreal on 22 May 1958. Ports of call en route were usually Cherbourg, Southampton, Cobh (Cork) and Quebec. During the winter season, *Arkadia* made cruises from England to the Canary Islands.

In 1961, *Arkadia* received her last refit at Blohm & Voss. She left the yard at 20,648 gross tons and with a capacity for 50 first class and 1,337 tourist class passengers. However, tighter Canadian immigration laws and a contraction of eastbound traffic led Greek Line to withdraw her from service in 1966. She made her last departure from Bremen on 16 August and from Montreal on 26 August. Upon arrival in England, she was laid up in the River Fal until she was sold to Spanish breakers in December 1966 and taken to Valencia on the 18th of that month to be broken up.

Queen of Bermuda

Builders Vickers-Armstrong Ltd, Barrow-in-Furness, 1933
Specifications 22,575 gross tons; 580 ft (177 m) long, 76 ft (23 m) wide
Machinery Steam turbo-electric; quadruple screw; speed 19 knots
Passengers 700 first class, 31 second class
Demise Scrapped in 1966

Built as a replacement for *Bermuda* that burned in Hamilton in June 1931 and was again undergoing repairs at Belfast in November, *Queen of Bermuda* took only 14 months to complete once the contract was signed by Vickers. She was finished on 14 February 1933, and departed from New York for Hamilton as Furness' flagship on 7 March 1933.

Though slightly larger than her sister ship *Monarch of Bermuda*, the two were practically the same. *Queen of Bermuda* had three funnels, the aftermost being a dummy, two masts, a grey hull and a counter stern. The only exterior differences between the two were that *Queen of Bermuda* had more cowl ventilators on her upper deck, three sets of suite windows below her promenade deck and her after promenade deck windows were not paired but arranged individually. As in the 'Monarch', *Queen of Bermuda's* public rooms were located on A-Deck and included the Homer Library, Forum Lounge, Osiris Verandah Cafe and the Elysium Dancing Hall. Aft was her only swimming-pool, the Silver Lagoon. Above on Sun Deck were the Gallery for the Forum, the de luxe cabins and the Corona Smoke Room. On D-Deck, accessible by three lifts was the Atrium Dining Room.

For the next six years, *Queen of Bermuda* and *Monarch of Bermuda* became affectionately known as the 'millionaires' ships', able to carry 4,500 passengers every three weeks on the New York-Bermuda run. Such 'millionaires' could enjoy a six-day cruise, that departed on either Saturdays (*Monarch*) or Wednesdays (*Queen*) in 1936 for as little as £10 ($50) for an inside cabin

Queen of Bermuda *sails out of New York on another six-day cruise* (Furness, Withy & Company).

with private facilities or as much as £51 ($250) for a de luxe suite. Both vessels proved themselves tremendous dollar earners.

At the outbreak of war in September 1939, *Queen of Bermuda* was hurriedly painted grey in New York harbour, then departed at top speed for Britain. There she was requisitioned by the Royal Navy and taken to Harland & Wolff, Belfast, for conversion into an armed merchant cruiser. Her luxury fittings were stripped and her decks were strengthened and provided with armour to which guns were fitted. In 1940 her third funnel and both masts were removed; in

their place were fitted a light tripod abaft the bridge and a small 'main' for wireless aerials in the third funnel position. Vents were replaced by mushroom-headed trunks and gun-pits mounted with AA armament were fitted abreast of the bridge, the second funnel and the after end of the superstructure. Finally, a spotter seaplane was carried aft on a thwart-ship catapult with a crane on the starboard side for lifting it back on board. Painted grey, *Queen of Bermuda* was employed on general convoy escort duties as well as patrolling for enemy surface raiders in the South Atlantic. On one such escort duty, she shielded a liner in which the King of Greece was travelling from South Africa to England. In 1943, she returned to

Above Queen of Bermuda *sailed as a two-stacker during the Second World War* (Furness, Withy & Company).

Below *The single-funnel* Queen of Bermuda *docking at Hamilton* (Furness, Withy & Company).

England and was converted into a troopship for 4,500 men. Her activities were world-wide, but she was principally occupied in the Middle East and off India and Burma. When the Queen finished her military duty, she had steamed 370,000 miles as an armed merchant cruiser and troop-ship, and carried 97,000 troops in her latter role from 1943 to 1947.

Queen of Bermuda was de-commissioned in April 1947 and handed back to Furness, who immediately sailed her to Harland & Wolff for a £3 million reconversion back to a luxury liner. During her 20-month refit, all of her public rooms were modernized and fitted with air-conditioning, additional cabins were fitted and the crew's accommodation was enlarged. De-

spite the alterations, her tonnage was reduced to 22,501 gross tons and her passenger capacity was listed as 682 first class and 49 second class. The third funnel was refitted and all were now stepped in ascending height like those of *Queen Mary*.

Queen of Bermuda resumed her New York-Bermuda shuttle run on 12 Febuary 1949. In 1951 Furness provided the *Queen* with the 13,654-ton consort *Ocean Monarch*. Times were different, and an American middle class with a discretionary income for travel was beginning to emerge. In 1955, a person sailing on a six-day Bermuda cruise in *Queen of Bermuda* paid from £45 ($125) to £179 ($500).

Furness was also beginning to feel the competition from the airlines, and taking into account *Queen of Bermuda*'s age, decided it was time for a refit. In October 1961, she was taken to Harland & Wolff at Belfast for a five-month

The Forum Lounge on board Queen of Bermuda *after 1963* (Furness, Withy & Company).

Queen of Bermuda*'s Corona Smoke Room* (Furness, Withy & Company).

major refit. Modifications included the fitting of a new raked stem, adding 9 ft to her overall length, making her 591 ft (180 m), the removal of her first and third funnels, the streamlining of her second stack and the replacement of her eight boilers by three. The forward boiler room was given over to a new air-conditioning plant and evaporator system capable of producing 150 tons of drinking water a day from sea water. Her 22,552 tons now accommodated 735 first class passengers.

Sporting her new profile, the rejuvenated *Queen of Bermuda* resumed her six-day Bermuda sailings on 7 April 1962. After such an invest-ment, it was presumed that she would last another ten years, but times had changed. Increasing operating costs rendered the Bermuda service unprofitable (this was primarily a problem of an ageing ship unable to comply with newer safety laws), and instead of investing money in new tonnage, Furness, to the surprise of the maritime world decided to call it a day. *Ocean Monarch* was withdrawn from service in September 1966, and on 19 November 1966 *Queen of Bermuda* made her last Bermuda sailing from New York. Sold to Shipbreaking Industries Ltd for £225,000, she arrived at Faslane on 6 December to be broken up, bringing to an end the passenger activity of Furness Bermuda Line. Ironically, her former sister ship, Greek Line's *Arkadia*, arrived in Spain that same month to be scrapped.

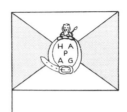

Hamburg-America Line (HAPAG)

Augusta Victoria

(Auguste Victoria, Kuban)

Builders Vulcan AG, Stettin, 1889
Specifications 7,661 gross tons; 463 ft (141 m) long (bp), 56 ft (17 m) wide
Machinery Triple expansion engines; twin screw; speed 18 knots
Passengers 400 first class, 120 second class, 580 third class
Demise Scrapped in 1907

Under the able direction of Albert Ballin, Hamburg Amerikanische Packetfahrt Aktien Gessel-schaft (HAPAG) placed orders for four twin-screw steamers for the Hamburg-New York express service. The first order was placed in 1887 with Vulcan AG and laid down as the *Normannia*. She was completed in 1889 as the *Augusta Victoria*, and was followed later that year

At the time of her completion, Augusta Victoria *was the largest ship built in a German yard* (Everett E. Viez, SSHSA Collection).

by her sistership, *Columbia*, and the larger *Normannia* and *Furst Bismarck* in 1890.

Augusta Victoria represented many 'firsts' for HAPAG. At the time of her completion, she was the largest liner to be built in a German yard. She was also the first to use the new buff funnel colours of HAPAG, and their first ship to be sent cruising.

Safety was an important selling point, and her all-important trio of buff funnels guaranteed the travelling public a trouble-free voyage. Concerning construction of the quartet, a HAPAG brochure stated 'the first consideration which the builders had in view was safety . . . and they have built ships which are practically unsinkable'. Each ship had a double bottom, and all working machinery was duplicated—two sets of boilers, two engines, two shafts and two screws, both sets working independently of each other and separated by a solid longitudinal bulkhead running from the keel to Upper Deck, dividing the vessel into two non-communicating halves, each of which was fully equipped

to propel the ship. Further, each side was subdivided into numerous watertight compartments.

On 10 May 1889, *Augusta Victoria* commenced her maiden voyage from Hamburg. She reintroduced a call at Southampton after a lapse of twenty years, then dashed across the Atlantic in 7 days 12 hours 30 minutes—then a record for a maiden voyage. For seven days, first-class passengers were treated to sumptuous accommodation illuminated by Edison's incandescent lamps.

Activity was centred on Promenade and Upper Decks. The former ran almost the entire length of the ship and included a Ladies' Salon 26 ft long and 17 ft wide located well forward with large oil paintings, mirrors and rich hangings of silks and damask. There was also a music-room exquisitely furnished and upholstered in silk of delicate tints, with furniture finished in white and gold, and a smoking-room whose walls were inlaid with porcelain panels of different designs complete with humorous mottoes and emblems carved in wood. Also located on this deck were a number of fine staterooms.

On Upper Deck was the main saloon decorated with a glass cupola; HAPAG described this room as 'simply perfect'. 'Everything about the ship has a military air. *Augusta Victoria's* dining-room extended through two decks, and passengers descended by a rococo staircase illuminated by starlike lights held by gilded cherubs. The stewards enter in regular order, and when a change is ordered they march out, keeping time to the band, with their neat uniforms and snow-white gloves, a goodly sight to see.' Were the stewards in training for the German Navy?

Second class accommodation was on the same decks as the first class, but at the after end. On Promenade Deck was 'a tastefully fitted Ladies' Room and a comfortable smoking room'. The main saloon on Upper Deck measured 40 ft by 36 ft and was artistically furnished, well lit and ventilated. At nine o'clock in the evening, the ship's band gave a concert there which was also attended by first class passengers. Cabins were commodious, being well furnished and with provision for both air and light. Bathrooms

with hot and cold water were also provided.

One of the problems confronting Ballin was how to utilize this express tonnage during what he predicted would be lean winter seasons. Looking over the discarded plans of Robert M. Sloman, Ballin took up the former's idea of sending a ship on a sightseeing excursion around the Mediterranean. He presented this idea to HAPAG's board of directors but they were unenthusiastic and dubious. Ballin nonetheless overruled his colleagues, put out advertisements for a cruise departing from Hamburg on 22 January 1891 in *Augusta Victoria* and hoped for the best. The magic day arrived, 241 sightseers stepped aboard, including Ballin and his wife, and *Augusta Victoria* cast off the Gibraltar, Genoa, Alexandria, Jaffa, Beirut, Constantinople, Athens, Malta, Naples and Lisbon. The cruise was a social and economic success, and an educational adventure. Additional cruises by *Augusta Victoria* or one of the other ships (*Columbia*, *Normannia* or *Furst Bismarck*) were subsequently scheduled out of New York or Hamburg every

year until the outbreak of the First World War.

Itinerary changes were introduced for *Augusta Victoria* in 1894 when HAPAG switched her to the Genoa-New York run; however, two years later she was placed back on the Hamburg-Southampton-New York route. During the winter of 1896-97, *Augusta Victoria* was taken to Harland & Wolff, Belfast, to be lengthened. She emerged from the yard 521 ft (159 m) long, with a tonnage of 8,479 gross tons, two masts instead of three and her name corrected to *Auguste Victoria*.

She resumed sailing between Hamburg, Southampton and New York on 3 June 1897, although occasionally when demand warranted it she was placed on the Genoa-New York route. *Auguste Victoria's* final transatlantic sailing from Hamburg tok place on 16 January 1904. Upon her return, the liner was sold to the Russians; they renamed her *Kuban* and operated her as an auxiliary cruiser. Her end came in 1907 when the fifteen-year-old Atlantic veteran was scrapped at Stettin.

Columbia

(Rapido, Terek)

Builders Laird Bros, Birkenhead, 1889
Specifications 7,363 gross tons; 463 ft (141 m) long (bp), 56 ft (17 m) wide

Auguste Victoria after her winter 1896-97 refit (C. A. Penrose/SSHSA Collection).

Machinery Triple expansion engines; twin screw; speed 18 knots
Passengers 400 first class, 120 second class, 580 third class
Demise Scrapped in 1907

Columbia was delivered to HAPAG in July 1889, and she was dispatched from Hamburg on the 18th of that month for Southampton and New York, and together with *Augusta Victoria* proved to be a great success.

Columbia was switched to the Genoa-Naples-New York route, but within a year was again serving the Channel ports. However, when demand necessitated tonnage in the Mediterranean, *Columbia*, along with her sister *Augusta Victoria*, was redirected accordingly.

The interiors of *Columbia* and *Augusta Victoria* were identical and quite elaborate for their day. There were electric lights, and first class passengers could summon their cabin steward at the push of a button.

During the Spanish-American War in 1898, *Columbia* was handed over to Spain who renamed her *Rapido* and operated her as an auxiliary cruiser. The war was of short duration, and *Rapido* was handed back to HAPAG the following year, and her name changed back to *Col-*

umbia. Her paintwork and interiors were touched up, then she resumed her transatlantic duties on the Hamburg-Southampton-New York and Genoa-Naples-New York routes.

With newer, bigger tonnage (the 'Pennsylva-nia' Class and the speed queen *Deutschland*) in the line, HAPAG decided to retire *Columbia*. She was sold in 1904 and became the Russian auxiliary cruiser *Terek*. Three years later she was scrapped.

Below *HAPAG's* Columbia (Alex Shaw, SSHSA Collection).

Bottom Columbia *undergoing refurbishment* (Hapag-Lloyd AG).

Normannia

(Patriota, L'Aquitaine)

Builders Fairfield Shipbuilding & Engineering
Co Ltd, Glasgow, 1890
Specifications 8,250 gross tons; 500 ft (152 m)
long (bp), 57 ft (18 m) wide
Machinery Triple expansion engines; twin
screw; speed 19 knots
Passengers 420 first class, 172 second class, 700
third class
Demise Scrapped in 1906

Normannia and her sister, *Furst Bismarck*, were
slightly larger versions of *Augusta Victoria* and
Columbia. Catering for a large first and third class
clientele, HAPAG's new flagship, *Normannia*,
departed Hamburg for New York on 22 May
1890.

HAPAG spared nothing in decorating *Normannia* and the three other ships, which were all
finished to the same standard. All were equipped
with the latest in technology and built with
safety in mind. Illumination was by Edison's
incandescent lamps and first class passengers
summoned their steward with an electric bell. As
in *Augusta Victoria*, *Normannia's* public rooms

were situated on two decks and contained a
ladies' saloon, a music-room with a Steinway
grand piano and a smoking-room—all easily
accessible from inside passageways. In some of
this latest quartet's predecessors, access to public
rooms had meant going outside in all weathers.
On Upper Deck was the main saloon that measured 72 ft by 40 ft. It was topped by a glass
cupola and the selected decor was late Renaiss-
ance, using a combination of dark woods and
gold; it also contained an upright piano. As on
their sisterships, the military air prevailed on
Normannia and *Furst Bismarck*.

The brochure stated that '. . . all accommodations for second-class passengers are on the same
deck as the first class'. The entire after Promenade Deck was devoted to their use, and they
had a fine selection of tastefully fitted public
rooms—a ladies' room, smoking-room and a
main saloon that measured 40 ft by 36 ft.

Normannia was deployed on the Genoa-
Naples-New York run in 1897, coinciding with
the arrival of the 12,000-ton 'Pennsylvania' Class
steamers, and the following year she was sold to
Spain, in whose ownership she served as the
auxiliary cruiser *Patriota*. The next year, she was
passed to French Line which was seeking a

Left *Flagship of HAPAG
for 12 months was* Normannia *(Hapag-Lloyd AG).*

Right Furst-Bismarck *at
anchor (Hapag-Lloyd AG).*

replacement for its *La Bourgogne*, sunk in a collision in July 1898 with the loss of 549 souls. As French Line's *L'Aquitaine*, she carried 432 first, 162 second and 2,000 third class passengers on the Le Havre-New York route. In this capacity, she sailed until September 1905, making 33 round trips to Le Havre. In 1906 she was sold and scrapped at Bo'ness.

Furst Bismarck

(Don, Moskva, Gaea, San Giusto)

Builders Vulcan AG, Stettin, 1891
Specifications 8,474 gross tons; 502 ft (153 m) long (bp), 57 ft (17 m) wide
Machinery Triple expansion engines; twin screw; speed 19 knots
Passengers 420 first class, 172 second class, 700 steerage
Demise Scrapped in 1924

The completion of *Furst Bismarck* fulfilled Ballin's ambition for a quartet of express steamers first envisaged in 1887. *Furst Bismarck* was HAPAG's lavish new flagship and made her maiden voyage from Hamburg on 8 May 1891,

calling at Southampton then steaming for New York. With the commissioning of *Furst Bismarck*, Hamburg-America was able to advertise a weekly express service from Hamburg utilizing 'four magnificent TWIN SCREW steamships' with rates for the 1893 summer season starting at £18 ($90) in a first class cabin and £12 ($60) in a second class cabin. Within a year, *Furst Bismarck* was placed on HAPAG's Mediterranean-New York service with a few winters spent cruising the warmer climates.

In 1904 *Furst Bismarck* was sold to the Russians and became the auxiliary cruiser *Don*. Two years later, she was handed over to the Russian Volunteer Fleet and renamed *Moskva*. Painted in the funnel colours of orange-buff with black tops, the flagship of RVF departed Libau (Latvia) for Rotterdam and New York on 13 May 1907. Four round trips were made, the last departing Libau on 23 December. *Moskva* then disappeared from commercial activity, presumably performing domestic work for the Russian Navy.

She reappeared in 1913 as *Gaea*, a depot ship for the Austrian Navy; in 1918 she was seized by Italy, turned over to Cosulich Line and renamed *San Giusto*. The ageing liner was rebuilt to carry 400 cabin and 1,400 third class passengers, and,

Above Furst Bismarck *under way* (Albert E. Gryer, SSHSA Collection).

Below *An eagle at her prow,* Imperator *is manoeuvred into her Hoboken pier* (Frank O. Braynard Collection).

after being repainted, departed from Trieste on 22 January 1921, arriving at New York on 10 February with 238 cabin and 1,137 third class passengers. Upon her return to Trieste she was laid up, and three years later was scrapped by Italian breakers.

Imperator

(Berengaria)

Builders Vulcan AG, Hamburg, 1913
Specifications 52,117 gross tons; 909 ft (277 m) long, 98 ft (30 m) wide
Machinery Steam turbines; quadruple screw; speed 23 knots
Passengers 908 first class, 972 second class, 942 third class, 1,772 steerage
Demise Scrapped in 1938/1946

Albert Ballin, the guiding light of Hamburg-America Line, decided to leave his Bremen rival, North German Lloyd, in the dust and put the British to shame by building a trio of giant liners. These would not be speed queen competitors, but instead would be the largest and most opulent vessels afloat. Slips were made ready at Vulcan and Blohm & Voss and the first keel was laid in June 1910. Tentatively named *Europa*, the first giantess was launched as *Imperator* on 23 May 1912 by Kaiser Wilhelm, the ship's patron. The second, *Vaterland*, followed on 3 April 1913, with *Bismarck* taking to the water on 20 June 1914. Ballin's plan was to have a weekly express de luxe steamer service between Cuxhaven and

The first class Dining Room on board Imperator *complete with white-tie stewards and musicians* (Hapag-Lloyd AG).

Left *Mewes' masterpiece, Imperator's Pompeian Pool* (Hapag-Lloyd AG).

Below right *All the comforts of home are to be found in this spacious first class cabin in* Imperator (Hapag-Lloyd AG).

Below *The pillarless Social Hall on* Imperator (Hapag-Lloyd AG).

New York established by 1915. All was on schedule until the First World War intervened.

Ballin summoned the best architects to Germany to work on the interiors of this big trio. The two most prominent were Cesar Ritz of Paris Ritz hotel fame whose name became synonymous with grandeur, and Charles Mewes, who, after 1905, became HAPAG's resident architect. Their first maritime product, HAPAG's *Amerika* of 1905, became the most fashionable ship on the Atlantic until the arrival of *Lusitania*.

Charles Mewes chose from the best aspects of eighteenth-century France for the interiors of *Imperator*. Her first class passenger entrance hall was situated on F-Deck and measured 95 ft wide by 69 ft long. Facing aft in the hall was the dining saloon with large windows and an elaborate, lofty glass dome above the galley on D-Deck. One deck down was one of Mewes' masterpieces, the Pompeian pool, modelled from the Royal Automobile Club original in London.

Though smaller in scale, *Imperator's* version was supported by Doric columns and accented with an imperial fountain and marble seats. It had a double staircase at one end giving access to a balcony running the length of the room. Passengers had the option of walking up or taking one of the two lifts to B-Deck.

B-Deck was Mewes' *tour de force*. Forward there were eight staterooms, followed by a curving staircase, a hall and then the smoking-room. Heading aft on either side of the first funnel casting was the lounge, or, as the Germans called it, the Social Hall, where all passengers, both men and women, could gather to have tea, talk, play cards or dance. This pillar-free chamber was 100 ft long, with ceilings hung from a series of girdered trusses overhead and complete with a skylight. Out in the 'foyer' were lifts and a stairway. Behind the second funnel casting was the Winter Garden. Mewes chose to decorate this room in gold and white, and chairs in sets of four and six were grouped around circular tables. The

central aisle led up a short flight of steps to a stage and within its proscenium were massive columns, wrought-iron railings and an extensive use of mahogany and gilt. To the immediate left at the landing was space for a string orchestra that played for passengers in the Winter Garden or dinner guests in the Ritz Carlton. Epicures patronizing this latter optional facility chose their own hours and selected their dishes cooked and served by a special staff of chefs and waiters from the Ritz Carlton Hotel in London. Diners made the grand entrance by ascending the stairs, while down below in the Winter Garden the other passengers participated in the ritual as if lounging in a Parisian pavement cafe. A-Deck, the sun deck of *Imperator*, was devoted to promenading and steamer chairs. In fine weather the lifeboats were swung outboard to give additional space so that passengers could have ample rom to play deck games.

On C-Deck were two palatial 'Imperial' suites. Each consisted of two bedrooms, two bathrooms, a breakfast-room, saloon, pantry, trunk-room, two servants' rooms and a private deck,

and each was available in 1913 for £1,028 ($5,000). Other cabins, if not as spectacular, were more than comfortable. Each first class stateroom had a marble wash-stand with hot and cold watertaps.

In the aftermath of the *Titanic* disaster, HAPAG went to great pains to reassure the travelling public about the safety of its new flagship. Among the safety features incorporated in *Imperator* were a steel double bottom, longitudinal and transverse bulkheads reaching far above the water line and a submarine bell signalling system, perhaps anticipating the global conflict. There were also searchlights of 34,000 candle power, lifeboats for all with room to spare, two motor launches with their own wireless telegraph on board, a gyro-compass and wireless telegraph with three telegraph operators on duty in turn. There was one commandant and

Ballin had a tendency to spoil passengers who travelled in the lower classes—this is the third class dining room of Imperator *(Hapag-Lloyd AG).*

four captains (for navigation, public safety and two for general superintendence).

Before *Imperator* departed for trials, an enormous crate arrived from Berlin at the fitting-out pier. It contained a huge gilt bronze eagle executed by Professor Bruno Kruse. The eagle had outstretched wings and a crown on its head, and in its claw it gripped a globe of the world on which was inscribed HAPAG's motto 'Mein Feld ist die Welt'. This object was incorporated into the bow of the liner, and gave her an extra 10 ft. It has often been argued that the Germans needed the extra 10 ft to maintain *Imperator's* size superiority over Cunard's new-built *Aquitania*.

On her way down the Elbe River in May 1913, *Imperator* went aground. Additional tugs were summoned and she was freed without damage on the next tide. At Cuxhaven, a workman having filled his lighter from a storeroom tin of benzene tried it out and started a flash fire. The blaze was confined to that compartment, but it took the life of five men. The maiden voyage was postponed and HAPAG blamed inadequate docking facilities at Cuxhaven for the delay. What they really feared was adverse publicity in the wake of the *Titanic* disaster. Repairs were made, and *Imperator* was made ready to sail for New York.

Under the command of Commodore Hans Ruser, *Imperator* sailed from Cuxhaven on 10 June 1913. After calls at Southampton, where she was given a cordial welcome, and Cherbourg, *Imperator* headed westward with 3,200 passengers, the largest maiden voyage complement. She arrived in New York 6 days 5 hours 12

Imperator after her winter 1913 refit with shortened funnels and no eagle. New York City's skyline forms the backdrop (Frank O. Braynard Collection).

minutes later to a traditional harbour welcome and docked at Hoboken, New Jersey (where all HAPAG ships docked prior to the First World War) across the Hudson River from New York. The happy passengers trooped ashore commenting how steady she was and that even in ' . . . fairly bad weather on this voyage there was very little motion'.

Misfortune struck *Imperator* again, however, while she was docked at Hoboken in September 1913. An indicator on the bridge alerted the officer on watch to smoke in the dry-stores room forward on the starboard side near the water line. The fire was contained to the area when the officer closed off the compartment, but firemen were rushed to the scene and stewards dispatched to wake the 'sleeping' immigrants. It was doubtful whether they need waking as they were quartered by the coaling ports, but, once the confusion died down, all were whisked to safety. The fire was eventually extinguished, but with the room in 30 ft of water, the liner began to list ominously towards the pier. Work parties were sent to clean up and *Imperator* departed for Germany two days behind schedule.

Once the thrill of sailing in the largest ship in the world faded, passengers on subsequent voyages were willing to articulate *Imperator's* chief problem. She was deficient in initial stability—in short, top heavy. This was hinted at earlier in May 1913, but nothing was done or could be done. Part of the problem lay within the lifesaving apparatus, the lifeboats. When *Titanic* sank, new regulations stated that lifeboats must be provided for all. In *Imperator's* case, 'all' meant over 5,000 souls. Room was therefore made for eighty-three lifeboats, half placed on the boat deck and the rest placed in bays carved out of the after shelter deck.

When *Imperator* entered New York with her bunkers empty and immigrants rushing to one side to see the Statue of Liberty, she listed horribly and Frahm's anti-rolling tanks designed to discourage rolling could do little to correct it. In fact, she 'hung on a roll' so much that New York's Sandy Hook pilots re-christened her the 'Limperator'. Her stability was improved during her winter at Vulcan yard when 9 ft was removed from the top of each funnel and the grill room with all its heavy furnishings was removed

and replaced with a veranda cafe open to the weather with cane furniture. More wicker was also introduced into the rooms and two thousand tons of cement were added as permanent ballast. The eagle stayed.

Imperator recommenced sailing in the spring of 1914. On that first voyage, one day out of Cherbourg, she ran into a gale with winds up to ninety miles an hour. She rode out the storm in six hours, but the next morning four lifeboats had been washed away and the eagle had lost its wings. On arrival at Cuxhaven, the remains were removed and never replaced.

Imperator undertook her last commercial sailing under German ownership on 8 July 1914 from Hamburg. Upon her return to Germany,

As Berengaria, *she became Cunard's flagship of the 1920s, shown here leaving New York (Frank O. Braynard Collection).*

she remained safely laid up at Hamburg along with many other HAPAG ships. On 27 April 1919 she was surrendered to the United States. Operated by the Navy, USS *Imperator* entered service as a troop transport until laid up in August 1919. Then, after heated arguments between England and the United States over Ballin's trio, it was decided by both parties that England should have the liner. She was handed over to the Shipping Controller in February 1920 and in turn chartered to Cunard Line.

Imperator undertook her first post-war voyage on 21 February 1920 between Liverpool and New York. In June, her British terminal was switched to Southampton, with an immediate call at Cherbourg. Seeking compensation for its lost *Lusitania*, Cunard Line purchased *Imperator* in February 1921. Renamed *Berengaria*, wife of Richard the Lionheart, she plied the Atlantic as Cunard's flagship until 1936.

Berengaria received an extensive refit from October 1921 to May 1922 at Armstrong, Whitworth & Co at Walker-on-Tyne. Her coal-burning engines were converted to oil-firing and to make her more stable all her lifeboats were placed on Boat Deck, all the marble in the first class suites was replaced with galvanized iron and an additional thousand tons of pig iron were added as permanent ballast. The converting of lifeboat bays into passenger space and other modifications led to her tonnage being increased to 52, 226 gross tons. To placate superstition, all cabins marked '13' were renumbered, and her capacity was reduced from a total of 4,594 to 970 first class, 830 second class and 1,000 third class passengers.

Among the first class public rooms to take on an English air were the Smoke Room, whose walls were now genuine brick and half-timbering in the Elizabethan manner complete with a coal-fired fireplace. The Lounge, the former Social Hall, was now panelled in walnut and the former Winter Garden was converted into the Palm Court with marble-topped tables. Finally, the former Ritz Carlton now became the Ballroom with a new parquet floor and marble columns. The only rooms to keep their original decor were the Pompeian Pool and the gymnasium. Of her hundreds of staterooms, only 157 had private bathrooms. In first class, they were modern and well-ventilated and a few had electrically-lighted closets.

Cunard took full advantage of its flagship's three stacks. They issued a booklet on the ship that stated 'Her three titanic red and black funnels are symbols of the adventures of other lands, other languages, other people'. With that, *Berengaria* resumed transatlantic sailings in company with *Mauretania* and *Aquitania*, making Cunard among the first to achieve a three-ship express service. Though *Mauretania* and *Aquitania* were superb running mates, it was the gleaming and bejewelled *Berengaria* that garnered for Cunard the rich and titled. Among some of her prominent passengers' were 'Lord Renfrew', in reality His Royal Highness the Prince of Wales, Lord and Lady Louis Mountbatten, the Sultan of Jahore, Lord Duveen, the Earl of Warwick, New York's Mayor Jimmy Walker, Will Rogers, Douglas Fairbanks, Henry Ford, J. P. Morgan and many Cortlands, DuPonts, Astors and Vanderbilts.

The United States immigration quota laws were firmly established by the mid-twenties, and Cunard, taking note of the new eastbound traveller, adjusted *Berengaria*'s passenger figures in May 1926 to 972 first class, 630 second class, 606 third class and 515 tourist class. In that year, one way first class was priced at £65 ($315) without facilities to £498 ($2,420) for an outside Parlour suite. The Imperial or Prince of Wales Suites cost £1,222 ($5,940) for one to four persons. Class descriptions changed in October 1931 to first, tourist and third, and finally, in February 1936, to cabin, tourist and third; in 1936, cabin fares started at £47 ($228) tourist at £27 ($135.50) and third class cost a flat £19 ($95).

During the early 1930s, passenger volume had dropped and to increase patronage and possibly make a profit, companies sent their liners cruising. The stately *Berengaria* was no exception. During the early 'thirties she was sent on $50 'booze cruises' in the lean autumn, winter and spring months, and by the mid-'thirties summers were also included. In 1935, *Berengaria* made five 13-day Caribbean cruises with rates starting at $125. A four-day Labor Day cruise to Bermuda in 1936, cost a minimum of £10 ($50) and in the

Berengaria *heading out to sea* (Frank O. Braynard Collection).

same year five-day New Year cruise cost £16 ($77.50) for an inside four-berth cabin, £18 ($90) for an inside cabin with shower and toilet and £47 ($230) for a Parlour suite. Her early cruising days earned her the nicknames of 'Bargain Area' and, later on, 'Dead and Bury'er'.

Cunard's intention was to keep *Berengaria* in operation until the arrival of the new *Queen Elizabeth*, scheduled for a 1940 delivery. *Berengaria*, however, was always plagued with small electrical fires, and on one occasion while at sea in the late 1920s it was serious enough to warrant passengers being told to report to their boat stations. Her final fire occured in her cabin class lounge on 3 March 1938 while she was at her pier in New York. In consequence, she returned to Southampton without passengers, was laid up and, before the end of the year, was sold to

shipbreakers at Jarrow. The former flagship was broken up all but her double bottom, the scrapping of which was completed in 1946 at Rosyth.

Vaterland

(Leviathan)

Builders Blohm & Voss, Hamburg, 1914
Specifications 54,282 gross tons; 948 ft (289 m) long, 100 ft (31 m) wide
Machinery Steam turbines; quadruple screw; speed 23.5 knots
Passengers 752 first class, 535 second class, 850 third class, 1,772 steerage
Demise Scrapped in 1938

The intended name for Ballin's second great liner was *Europa*, but the international crisis in Europe made it more expedient for Prince Rupert of Bavaria to christen her *Vaterland* on 3 April 1913.

This was the second time that a ship had been christened by a man (the first was *Imperator*), a role almost universally accorded to women. After a year of fitting out, the largest ship in the world was completed. Hamburg-America was able to claim that it was the largest steamship company in the world, possessing 442 steamers totalling 1,417,710 tons.

HAPAG's marine architect, Charles Mewes, managed to persuade the naval architects to divide the boiler uptakes on each side of the superstructure so he could design a series of public rooms along the central axis, a thus unobstructed 391 ft long space. The results along B-Deck were spectacular. At the extreme front were five cabins each with a private bath. Just aft of these was a library, then a hall containing a grand staircase. Continuing aft was the 75 ft long

Ballin's massive Vaterland *(Frank O. Braynard Collection).*

Social Hall. This pillarless room was entered from the sides and contained four oil paintings and a bust of the Kaiser himself. At the forward end, ascended by five steps, was an orchestra stage. Exiting aft through central doors, the next lounge the passengers entered was the Winter Garden, followed by a short flight of steps to the famed Ritz Carlton, copied exactly from the New York Ritz. Circumventing the after casting (the third funnel for engine-room ventilation), the Tea Room was entered via the enclosed promenade deck. The first class dining-room had a three-storey dome and Mewes created another masterpiece, the Pompeian pool on G-Deck.

As in *Imperator*, the other classes were also well provided for. Even steerage passengers had a separate dining-room, complete with its own kitchen and stewards—Ballin really outdid himself.

Technically, *Vaterland's* most distinctive features were the double bottom and watertight

Vaterland *in drydock* (Frank O. Braynard Collection).

Vaterland*'s Wintergarden and Ritz-Carlton Restaurant* (Hapag-Lloyd AG).

bulkheads (specially designed in light of the *Titanic* disaster), fireproof glass doors that could withstand a temperature of 1,000°, 84 lifeboats, two motor boats, a wireless with a 1,500 mile radius and a giant searchlight perched on the forward mast.

Hamburg-America had profited from the shortcomings of *Imperator*, and *Vaterland* emerged more streamlined and stable. She departed from Cuxhaven on her maiden voyage on 14 May 1914. After stops at Southampton and Cherbourg to embark additional passengers, HAPAG's flagship under the command of Commodore Hans Ruser steamed to New York (Hoboken) with 1,677 passengers. She arrived 5 days 17 hours later on 21 May and sailed up river from Quarantine escorted by no fewer than 25 tugs, which a HAPAG official deemed adequate.

Vaterland proceeded very slowly as a strong north wind and falling tide started to affect her manoeuvrability. Abreast of the pier, a string of Leight Valley barges cut across her bow. Whistles were blown and the ship put to 'Full Astern'; then, as the giant liner slid back downstream, she threatened another rail barge. The approach was attempted again and after five hours *Vaterland* was safely berthed. Among the distinguished passengers who disembarked where Adolph S. Ochs, co-owner of the *New York Times*, Nelson W. Aldrich, one of the founders of Citicorp, and Alexander W. Carlisle, the retired partner of Lord Pierrie of Harland & Wolff, Belfast. He said that '*Vaterland* was the most wonderful ship afloat, and he did not think that she would be surpassed in his time'.

Four days later, *Vaterland* left New York for her return voyage and she seemed determined to take revenge on the rail barges that impeded her arrival. At twelve sharp, she pulled smartly away from her Hoboken pier with full astern power, but when the engine telegraph was pulled to stop, *Vaterland* failed to respond. Well-wishers on the pier looked on in horror as the liner slid backwards across the river. Finally, with her stern actually between two Manhattan piers, her by now white-faced chief engineer managed to get steam admitted to the high-pressure turbines and the quadruple screws thundered forward. The turbulence, however, swamped a coal barge and damaged two others.

Vaterland completed only three round voyages. She commenced the fourth on 22 July 1914, and arrived at New York on 30 July, a few days before the outbreak of the First World War. Preparing to sail on 31 July, with 2,700 passengers, *Vaterland's* captain received a cable from Germany warning of British and French cruisers lying in ambush waiting to seize the ship outside New York. The captain promptly cancelled the sailing and awaited further instructions. The new liner was subsequently interned at New York (Hoboken) along with four other ships of the Hamburg-America Line.

When the United States entered the war in April 1917, *Vaterland*, along with other German vessels in US waters, was seized as a war prize and converted into a troop transport. However, before she could sail under the Stars and Stripes, repairs had to be made to the engines and boilers

Leviathan as a US Navy transport during the First World War. Notice the guns on her foredeck (Frank O. Braynard Collection).

following sabotage by the German crew. During the repair work the liner was renamed *Leviathan* in September 1917. The American flagship departed Hoboken with her first batch of 10,000 'doughboys' in December 1917. During the crossing, the cable on her steam whistle contracted with the cold, bellowing into the night and frightening the lads below! Upon arrival in Liverpool, she was dry-docked to be bottom cleaned and 'dazzle-painted' with a series of contrasting bands of black, white and grey paint. This concept was conceived by British Navy Officer and marine artist Norman Wikinson, who sought to puzzle the enemy as to what direction the ship was travelling. On another eastbound crossing in September 1918 with over 9,000 men aboard, an epidemic of 'flu broke out killing 91. In September 1919, the war over, *Leviathan* was laid up at Hoboken and handed over to the United States Shipping Board (USSB), a government agency connected with the Department of Commerce.

Leviathan's future remained cloudy while details of her ownership were established. During most of this time she was placed under the management of the International Mercantile Marine Company (IMM). This company was founded in 1902 by J. P. Morgan to monopolize shipping on the North Atlantic. William Randolph Hearst, the newspaper magnate, objected to this arrangement, since he considered IMM to be a British company. Hearst wanted *Leviathan* to be under a 'true' American company flying the

Leviathan in French waters (Frank O. Braynard Collection).

American flag so that in another emergency the liner would be readily available. With his financial resources, he managed to persuade Congress against a sale to IMM. Instead, *Leviathan* was placed under the red, white and blue colours of the newly formed United States Lines, created in August 1921.

Once the ownership question was settled, attention was turned to conversion. This was a formidable task. USSB did not possess the original plans of *Vaterland*, and when William Francis Gibbs went to Blohm & Voss to inquire about them he was quoted the exorbitant figure of $1 million. Naturally, the Germans were not disposed to be helpful; they were about to lose their *Bismarck*, and now the Americans had the audacity to request the original plans of *Vaterland*! William Gibbs returned to America, determined to make his own drawings. A team of naval draughtsmen scoured every inch of the liner, and when they finished twelve months later, Gibbs had a complete set of drawings which he presented to USSB. Once approved, a dry dock was prepared at Newport News and *Leviathan* headed south on 8 April 1922.

In charge of the $8,200,000 conversion were the Gibbs Brothers—William and Frederic—and their team of draughtsmen. *Leviathan* was re-wired, given oil-fired engines and strengthened. Accommodation was provided for 3,391 passengers—970 first class, 542 second class, 944 third class and 935 fourth class—and a crew of 1,115 to attend to their needs and navigate the giant across the ocean. During conversion, USL wanted to honour President Harding by renaming *Leviathan* after him, in keeping with its new policy of honouring US Presidents. Harding thought the gesture flattering but declined, since the 'Teapot Dome Scandal' that had broken in the autumn of 1923 would have placed United States Lines in an embarrassing position had it chosen his name. Teapot Dome was an oil reserve in Wyoming set aside for navy use, but when Albert Fall, Harding's Secretary of the Interior, received half a million dollars from two oil executives in return for secret leases allowing them to drill on the reserves for their private profit, the secret eventually leaked out and the scandal synonymous with Harding's administration ensued, involving this reserve and the one at Elk Hill, California.

The red, white and blue funnelled *Leviathan* emerged from Newport News in June 1923, and commenced trials. With clean, refitted engines, she managed to attain a speed of 28.54 knots, enabling her to be billed as the fastest liner in the world! Cunard promptly protested and USL later admitted that the speed was achieved with the Gulf Stream and the wind in *Leviathan's* favour. The flagship of the US merchant marine and the largest liner in the world at 59,956 gross tons arrived in New York to a tumultuous welcome. On Independence Day, 4 July 1923, under the command of Captain Herbert Hartley, *Leviathan* sailed from her Manhattan pier for Cherbourg and Southampton with 1,800 passengers. Her four screws connected to 46 boilers fed by 9,563 tons of fuel propelled her across the Atlantic in six days.

The American naval architects had striven for spaciousness, quiet elegance and beauty. On A-Deck forward was the smoking-room finished in English oak. One deck lower, on B-Deck, were five cabins with baths at the extreme forward end. Behind them was a library decorated in soft greys, blues and greens. Passing the grand staircase, next was the Social Hall with its French oak panelling, four huge decorative pictures and carpets copied from Persian rugs. Through the

lobby, the next room was the Winter Garden. Soaring columns with gold capitals, chairs and tables painted to tone with the walls, green lattice-work, curtains of gold and black together with clustered blossoms and graceful palms gave this room a tropical charm. At the top of a few steps, first class passengers entered the Ritz Carlton Room finished in the style of the Empire with carved mahogany, metalwork ornament and a frescoed ceiling. Further aft was the Tea Room. The dining-room was on F-Deck, and the theme was simplicity coupled with elegance. There were Grecian columns topped by arches of unusual beauty, and a painted dome surrounded by lights.

Second class passengers were allocated two public rooms (a social hall and smoking-room) on the after third of D-Deck, an enclosed promenade deck and a dining-room on F-Deck with tables seating from three to ten people. Third class was given two tiny rooms on the after end of D-Deck, some deck space and a dining-room with a long table at the after end of E-Deck. Fourth class was given space at the extreme forward end of the liner, as it had been on *Vaterland*. The best term to use to describe this accommodation was 'improved steerage'.

Together with *America*, *George Washington* and *Republic*, United States Lines had a viable first class fleet, but unlike Cunard and White Star Line, which had balanced three-ship fleets—*Berengaria*, *Mauretania*, *Aquitania*; *Olympic*, *Homeric*, *Majestic*—*Leviathan* had no consort. Another hindrance to *Leviathan's* success was the albatross of Prohibition that extended to American ships at sea as well as foreign ships within 12 miles of US territorial waters. Thus, American ships were dry, and thirsty Americans avoided them, preferring instead the open bars of foreign ships. It was no surprise that the new French liner of 1927, *Ile de France*, had the longest bar afloat! Finally, US immigration laws passed in the mid-'twenties hurt patronage for *Leviathan* and other ships, but despite these adversities, *Leviathan* sailed on, piling up deficits in USL's ledgers.

One of her most colourful captains was Commodore Herbert Hartley. He was a strict enforcer of the Prohibition laws, and during the

Docking the giant at New York (Frank O. Braynard Collection).

voyage he would gather together all the bottles of spirits and dump them in front of *Leviathan's* bow. Another of his activities was performing marriages, of which he conducted nine, on his special 'marriage rug'. He also had a sense of humour. During a severe spring gale in 1926, a deranged lady made her way forward and managed to gain access outdoors. She ascended a vertical ladder to the wheelhouse into which she was pulled by the startled Commodore and his officers. Her hair and clothes drenched and dripping, she asked 'How far are we from land?' The Commodore replied 'About three miles.' Later, in one of his throw-away lines, he added 'Land was three miles . . . straight down'. During an

eastbound crossing in December 1929, *Leviathan* encountered one of her worst storms. This one resulted in a one-inch crack on her starboard side going down 20 ft to C-Deck. She was out of service for three months undergoing repairs costing $700,000.

Since the only way to cross the Atlantic was by steamer, the *crème de la crème* flocked to the flagships, and *Leviathan* carried her share of noted personalities. Among the most regal was Queen Marie of Rumania, who voyaged in the liner westbound in October 1926 with her ladies in waiting, aides-de-camp and 90 trunks. Other prominent personages that graced *Leviathan* were Gloria Swanson, Douglas Fairbanks Snr, Mary Pickford, Cardinal Hayes, Rudolf Valentino, the Duke and Duchess of Richelieu, Maharajah Rajenda Bahadur of Jin and Mrs Whitelaw Reid, wife of the editor and publisher of the *New York Herald Tribune*. Gloria Swanson had a habit of keeping her pet Pekinese in her cabin and bringing him down to lunch and dinner in the dining-room, where the dog would help itself to choice morsels from the plates. When informed that *Leviathan* had a well-kept kennel, Miss Swanson responded 'there's not enough light for me to read it a bed-time story'. Within 24 hours the kennel was well lit and her pet was never seen at the table again.

Leviathan achieved a rather novel distinction in August 1927 when the first mail plan was flown off a liner. Carpenters in New York built a 100 ft ramp on top of *Leviathan's* teak bridge pointing diagonally over the portside of the flying bridge. The plane was poised at its after end. The flight took place on 1 August, when *Leviathan* was 80 miles east of Ambrose. The pilot, Clarence Chamberlin, climbed into his tiny Fokker bi-plane and once the deck-hands had mopped the 'runway', he revved up his engines and was airborne within 75 ft despite the fact that there was no catapult involved. The next vessel to try this stunt was *Ile de France* in August 1928.

Paul Wadsworth Chapman, a Chicago financier, purchased United States Lines in 1929, but the only change *Leviathan* witnessed was the restyling of her capacity. By April 1930, she could cater for 940 first class, 666 tourist class and 1,402 third class passengers. However, Chapman failed to honour his obligations and the company reverted to USSB, who in turn handed it over to a new organization, United States Lines Company, in 1931. This company immediately reduced *Leviathan's* tonnage from 59,956 to 48,932, even though not a single thing was added or removed from the liner—USLC simply switched to American measurements! This reduction allowed the company to save $40,000 a year in port charges, since these were based on a ship's tonnage.

The harsh economic realities of the depression forced USLC to put an end to their loss-making services by withdrawing *Leviathan*. She departed from Southampton on 17 December 1931, and on arrival in New York was laid up for the winter. On 26 April 1932, *Leviathan* commenced a series of 11 round voyages from New York to

Plymouth, Cherbourg, Bremen, Southampton and Cherbourg, after which she was again laid up. On 25 April 1933, she raised steam and made one round trip to England, France and Germany, then the following year she assisted *Manhattan* and *Washington* by making four round trips starting on 9 June. Each voyage cost the company $134,000 (approximately £27,750). Her arrival on 14 September at New York marked the end of her commercial activity; she was towed over to Hoboken and forgotten.

Leviathan started her last voyage on 26 January 1938. Under the command of Captain Binks and flying the red duster of the British Merchant Marine, she left the Hudson and moved out across the Atlantic to Rosyth to be scrapped. Reminiscent of her trooping days, the cold once again contracted the wire controlling the steam whistles and a series of ghostly blasts were triggered. *Leviathan* arrived at Rosyth on 14 February, bringing an end to one of Ballin's magnificent trio.

Bismarck

(Majestic, Caledonia)

Builders Blohm & Voss, Hamburg, 1914–1922
Specifications 56,551 gross tons; 956 ft (291 m) long, 100 ft (30 m) wide
Machinery Steam turbines; quadruple screw; speed 23.5 knots
Passengers 750 first class, 542 second class, 850 third class
Demise Scrapped in 1940–1943

The last of Ballin's opulent floating palaces was to have been christened by Bismarck's grand-daughter, Countess Hanna von Bismarck, on 20 June 1914, but when the Countess swung the bottle and missed, the ceremony was properly completed by the Kaiser who, standing by her side, caught the bottle and aimed better. Thus all three giants were launched by men. It is ironic that on coming to the imperial throne in 1888, one of the Kaiser's first acts had been to dismiss Bismarck as Chancellor.

Two months after the launching, work ceased on *Bismarck* for the duration of the war. On 28

June 1919, Germany signed the Treaty of Versailles under which *Bismarck* was handed over to Great Britain and placed under the management of the Shipping Controller. In a short time, refitting resumed at Blohm & Voss under British supervision. A terrible fire on 5 October 1920 added considerable delays to the fitting out, then in February 1921, *Bismarck* was purchased by White Star Line, while sistership *Imperator* was sold to Cunard. This joint purchase from the Shipping Controller was made to avoid the companies outbidding each other.

When *Bismarck* was completed on 28 March 1922, she sailed for Liverpool in Hamburg-America funnel colours, but with no flag flying. Leaving Liverpool on 1 April, she began ten days of sea trials, then, after the trials, White Star named its flagship and fastest ship *Majestic*. As regards tonnage, *Majestic's* sistership *Vaterland* entered service in 1914 at 54,282 gross tons, and emerged in 1923 as *Leviathan* at 59,956 tons, 3,405 tons more than *Majestic*. However, when it came to economize in 1931, United State Lines adopted the American standard of measurement and *Leviathan* was reduced to 48,932 tons. This settled the largest liner in the world argument and *Majestic* became number one.

Mewes and Davis (the latter worked on the interiors of *Aquitania*) had no hand in the decoration of *Majestic*. Mewes' only 'decorative' element were the uptakes divided along the sides of the superstructure, giving the White Star team a unobstructed central space in which to work. The layout of public rooms in *Majestic* was exactly the same as in *Leviathan*. There was a library, Lounge (*Majestic's* largest room) panelled in oak with French windows, Grand Foyer, Palm Court (decorated in a style similar to that of *Leviathan* but with fewer blossoms) and à la carte Restaurant. Above the library was the smoking-room. The dining-room was down below and was also decorated similarly to the American ship, except that the painted dome had four lights around it. The most outstanding features of Ballin's trio were their Pompeian Pools, and *Majestic's* was just as lavish.

The second class dining saloon sat 400 and, after eating, passengers could ascend to the lounge, reading-room or smoking-room by an electric lift. Third class had twice as much room in *Majestic* as in *Leviathan*; they were provided with a lounge, smoking-room and dining saloon.

Majestic had 1,245 staterooms, of which 472 were for first class, and she carried only 2,142 passengers. Regardless of class, White Star assured passengers that all public rooms and staterooms were heated by both steam and electricity, and that the ventilation system automatically guaranteed a constant supply of fresh air at the proper temperature to all parts of the ship.

Majestic raised steam on 10 May 1922, and,

Left Bismarck, *the last of Ballin's trio designed to drive the competition from the North Atlantic* (Hapag-Lloyd AG).

Right Majestic, *White Star's flagship of the 1920s, departing from New York* (Richard Morse Collection).

Below Majestic *in drydock at Southampton* (National Archives, Washington DC).

with Commodore Bertram Hayes in command, set sail from Southampton and Cherbourg on her maiden voyage to New York. For the next ten years, Majestic and her consorts, *Olympic* and *Homeric*, served on White Star's Southampton-Cherbourg-New York express service, but it was the three-stacker and flagship that sailed on to build the greatest reputation, securing for White Star their share of the celebrity market. In August 1922, an honour befell *Majestic* when King George V and Queen Mary paid a visit to the liner during Cowes Week at Southampton.

The Depression of the early 'thirties destroyed many shipping companies and those that survived diverted ships to other waters during the off season. The great *Majestic* was no exception. She too was sent on occasional cruises from New York to Nova Scotia and to Nowhere in a scheme to lure capital into White Star's coffers. At the same time, White Star was cutting back on staff; this resulted in reduced maintenance and service aboard the liners. On the verge of bankruptcy, White Star was forced to merge with financially-troubled Cunard and in 1934 *Majestic* was transferred to the newly-formed Cunard-White Star Line.

Lasting only two years under this new ownership *Majestic* commenced her last voyage on 13

Without her lifeboats and with shortened masts and funnels, Caledonia *sails for the scrapyards* (Frank O. Braynard Collection).

February 1936 from Southampton. When she arrived home she was laid up, and by May had been sold to T. W. Ward for scrapping. Stripped of most of her exterior fittings and with funnels cut down for the intended passage under Forth Bridge, *Majestic* was bought by the British Admiralty and refitted at Thornycroft, Southampton, for use as a training ship for 2,000 boys. On 8 April 1937, she sailed as HMS *Caledonia* for Rosyth, where she was permanently moored.

When the Second World War erupted in Europe, work began immediately on refitting *Caledonia* as a transport. On 29 September 1939, during conversion, a fire broke out on board and completely destroyed the liner. The superstructure was burned out and *Caledonia* sank on an even keel in shallow water. She was salvaged the following March, but proved to be beyond repair. Sold again to T. W. Ward in March 1940, work began to scrap the wreck on the spot. On 17 July 1943, the remainder of the wreck was raised and towed to Inverkeithing, where it was scrapped.

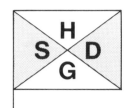

Hamburg-South America Line

Cap Trafalgar

Builders Vulcan AG, Hamburg, 1914
Specifications 18,805 gross tons; 613 ft (187 m) long, 72 ft (22 m) wide
Machinery Triple expansion engines; triple screw; speed 17 knots
Passengers 400 first class, 274 second class, 912 third class
Demise Sunk in 1914

A demand for suitable first class vessels to transport the wealthy to and from Europe was answered by Hamburg-South America Line when they ordered two large three-funnel liners, *Cap Trafalgar* and *Cap Polonio*. The first to be launched was *Cap Trafalgar* on 31 July 1913; she was completed in March 1914. On the 10th of that month, she set sail for Rio de Janeiro and

The only liner to be sunk by another liner was Cap Trafalgar (Hamburg-South America Line).

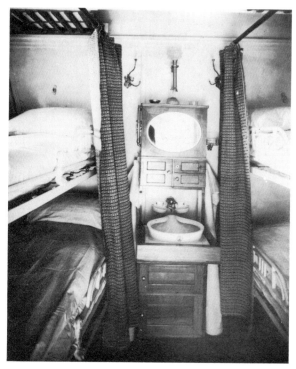

Above left *Second class smoking room aboard* Cap Trafalgar *(Hamburg-South America Line).*

Left *Second class dining room on* Cap Trafalgar *(Hamburg-South America Line).*

Above *A four-berth second class cabin on board* Cap Trafalgar *(Hamburg-South America Line).*

Buenos Aires. She was not only the flagship of Hamburg-South America, but also the largest and most luxurious ship to sail the South Atlantic.

On board was a Winter Garden which featured a series of terraces laid in yellow marble. These were interplanted with banks of tropical plants and flowers. Fountains played while tropical birds—parrots, macaws, and toucans—chattered from a series of perches and cleverly designed cages.

Cap Trafalgar was supposed to sail from Buenos Aires for Germany on 19 August 1914 with a full complement of passengers, but the war altered her plans. Under Kommandant Fritz Langerhannsz, she slipped her moorings in

Buenos Aires on 18 August with 60 passengers and a crew of 270. She headed for Montevideo, where she arrived the next morning. There, many of the passengers, ranging from children to grandmothers, were put ashore and additional bunkers loaded. With 3,500 tons of coal, piles of timber and the male members of an opera company who opted to remain as crew members, *Cap Trafalgar* was ordered by Berlin to report immediately to Trinidad Island, 1,750 miles from Montevideo. She sailed at midnight on 22 August.

To evade detection by British warships and to fool any British or Allied merchant ship that came into view, Kommandant Langerhannsz decided he must disguise his ship's silhouette, since she was the only three-funnel liner in the South Atlantic. What ship could she resemble? The Kommandant and one of his officers, Feddersen, decided on *Carmania*, since she was one of many British-built two-funnel 20,000-tonners. While under way, the crew of *Cap Trafalgar* removed her third dummy funnel, constructed a dummy bridge cut from backdrop scenes and stitched together a British ensign and Cunard house-flag. Thus disguised, the liner arrived at Trinidad Island on 28 August, where Captain Julius Wirth of the Imperial Marine assumed command.

Conversion into a cruiser commenced immediately, using the guns from the gunboat *Eber*. The armament consisted of two 10.5 cm guns and six machine-guns. Operational staff were 13 officers, five petty officers and 283 men. On 31 August 1914 she became an auxiliary cruiser and on 4 September left Trinidad Island.

Meanwhile, the real *Carmania* was under the command of Captain Noel Grant, and he was given orders to proceed from Trinidad, West Indies (which she left on 4 September) to Rio de la Plata, where she would be patrolling. On 13 September, *Carmania* received orders to inspect the Vas Rocks and Trinidad Island, suspected of being used by the Germans. *En route*, Captain Grant decided he must disguise his ship's silhouette so as to be able to observe closely the suspected German ship activities. He decided that since there was only one German 20,000-ton, three-funnel liner in the area, his vessel would have to take on the profile of that ship. Therefore, *Carmania's* crew erected a third dummy funnel.

Cap Trafalgar returned to Trinidad Island on 13 September. The next day, bunkering was interrupted when *Carmania* approached. The latter spotted a set of masts at 11.04 am while *Cap Trafalgar* steered a south-westerly course away from the oncoming intruder. *Carmania* fired the first shot across the other's bow. *Cap Trafalgar* then started to head directly at *Carmania*, on the way firing her guns. Both ships were soon ablaze, forcing *Carmania's* crew to abandon the destroyed bridge. Commander Lockyer of the British ship ran down the lines of guns shouting 'individual fire, aim for the water-line'. A succession of point-blank-range shells followed, smashing the plates along *Cap Trafalgar's* water-line. Within an hour the ships had separated, each burning, and *Cap Trafalgar* sinking. *Carmania* returned briefly and again guns were fired, but Captain Grant realized it was over. His ship finally disengaged from battle and headed for sea with no bridge, engine-room or steering controls.

A German collier, *Eleonore Wouvermans*, commanded by Langerhannsz provided a smoke screen for the dying German flagship, which was listing heavily to starboard. Captain Wirth, with a piece of bridge rail embedded in his left armpit, gave the order for the crew, but not the officers, to abandon ship. Abandonment completed, he dismissed his officers. *Eleonore Wouvermans* rescued 286 crew members; twelve had died in the battle and three were reported missing, presumably eaten by sharks. *Cap Trafalgar* lifted her stern into the air and slipped down into the deep South Atlantic Ocean, becoming the first and only passenger liner to be sunk by another passenger liner in armed conflict.

Cap Polonio

(Vineta)

Builders Blohm & Voss, Hamburg, 1919
Specifications 20,576 gros tons; 662 ft (202 m) long, 72 ft (22 m) wide
Machinery Triple expansion engines; twin

screw; speed 17 knots
Passengers 356 first class, 250 second class, 949 third class
Demise Scrapped in 1935

Laid down in 1913 as the larger sister of *Cap Trafalgar*, *Cap Polonio*, whose name was taken from the Cape between the border of Brazil and the Rio de La Plata on the coast of Uruguay, was launched on 25 March 1914. Five months later work was suspended due to the outbreak of war, and by the end of that year the German Navy found it advantageous to hurriedly fit the ship out as an auxiliary cruiser. Renamed *Vineta* and sporting two funnels (the third was removed during conversion), she entered service on 9 February 1915. Her slow speed of 17 knots did not make for a quick chase or escape, so the German high command decided to take her out of service, remove her armament and fit her out as originally intended, a three-funnel passenger ship. The work was completed in 1916 and her name reverted to *Cap Polonio*.

At the conclusion of hostilities, *Cap Polonio* was handed over to Britain in 1919. The Shipping Controller chartered her to Union Castle Line and she was given its funnel colours and departed from Plymouth on one round trip to Cape Town. However, her troublesome engines made her speed very poor. Handed back to the Shipping Controller, she was then chartered to P & O. Under its buff funnel colours, *Cap Polonio* made one round voyage to Bombay from London, after which she was laid up at Liverpool in 1919. On 20 July 1921, to the great satisfaction of Hamburg and the German people generally, she was sold to her original owner, Hamburg-South America Line, and on her return to Hamburg she received a great welcome.

Taken into Blohm & Voss, *Cap Polonio* was given an overhaul with particular attention being paid to her engines. They were converted to oil-firing, and during trials gave trouble-free performances.

On 16 February 1922, the citizens of Hamburg gave Hamburg-South America's flagship, the largest vessel on the route until 1926, a rousing send-off. Commodore Rolin guided his ship down the Elbe River whose banks were lined

Above Cap Polonio (Hamburg-South America Line).   **Below** Cap Polonio *steaming out of Hamburg* (Hamburg-South America Line).

with thousands of wildly cheering Germans. Once at sea, the Commodore pointed *Cap Polonio's* bow west and then south for Rio de Janeiro and Buenos Aires. Her initial voyage was everything her owners dreamed of, and she became a great success and a very popular liner on both sides of the Atlantic.

Like many other liners, *Cap Polonio* fell victim to the great world economic depression. With little first-class patronage, Hamburg-South America decided to lay up the ship at Hamburg. In September 1933, she was pulled out of retirement to serve as an Exhibition ship at the Hamburg Overseas Landing Stage, but once the fair was over she was once again laid up. With no future, *Cap Polonio* was sold for breaking up at Bremerhaven in June 1935.

Cap Arcona

Builders Blohm & Voss, Hamburg, 1927
Specifications 27,560 gross tons; 676 ft (206 m) long, 84 ft (27 m) wide
Machinery Steam turbines; twin screw; speed 20 knots

Passengers 575 first class, 275 second class, 465 third class
Demise Attacked and sunk in 1945

On 19 November 1927, *Cap Arcona* started her career as Hamburg-South America's flagship between Hamburg and Buenos Aires as the largest and fastest vessel on the South American route. This distinction was lost for a period of two years, between 1931 and 1933, when *L'Atlantique* was in service. Along with her consort, the smaller three-funnelled *Cap Polonio*, and numerous smaller ships in the 13,000-ton range, she helped Hamburg-South America provide a viable service for both immigrants and first-class passengers between northern Europe and South America.

Cap Arcona was known as the 'queen of the South Atlantic', and for good reason. Her speed enabled her to steam from Hamburg to Rio de Janeiro in 12 days and to Buenos Aires in 15, and during those days on board her first class passengers could enjoy the use of a heated indoor salt-water swimming-pool, a carpeted restaurant located on the upper promenade deck with twenty windows overlooking the sea, a lounge

Left *The Conservatory in* Cap Polonio (Hamburg-South America Line).

Right *Queen of the South Atlantic was* Cap Arcona (Hamburg-South America Line).

Below Cap Arcona *arriving in Hamburg* (Hamburg-South America Line).

Above Cap Arcona *at full speed. Note the yarning to guard against the hot sun* (Hamburg-South America Line).

Left *The Main Lounge aboard* Cap Arcona; *the potted plants give the room a tropical atmosphere* (Hamburg-South America Line).

Above right *A carpeted deck and carved wooden columns, not to mention flowers on each table, awaited the diners in* Cap Arcona's *first class dining room* (Hamburg-South America Line).

Right *The second class dining room of* Cap Arcona (Hamburg-South America Line).

adorned with potted plants, a complete gymnasium and a full-sized tennis court at the upper end of the promenade deck. After an exhausting day in the lap of luxury, they could retire to outside staterooms with private facilities, which in 1933 started at £89 ($357) to Rio and £100 ($400) to Buenos Aires. Second class to Rio was £46 ($185), third class (room) £27 ($110) and third class (deck) £24 ($97).

The outbreak of the Second World War found *Cap Arcona* safely at Hamburg. She remained there until 1940; then, in November of that year, she sailed to Gotenhafen (Gdynia) in Poland to become an accommodation ship. As the Russians made their westward march to Berlin, liberating German-occupied areas, the retreating armies decided in the late winter and early spring of 1945 to commission *Cap Arcona* as an evacuation ship. As such, she made three voyages, trans-porting 26,000 people from the German eastern territories to the west.

In April 1945, *Cap Arcona* embarked 5,000 prisoners from the Neuengamme concentration camp while the ship was off Neustadt in the Bay of Lubeck. If crew and guards are included in the count, there were 6,000 people aboard the liner. On 3 May, *Cap Arcona* was attacked with rockets and machine-gun fire by British fighter-bombers. She caught fire and panic broke out on board. Finally, the continued aircraft attack caused the ship to capsize. Despite the fact that the liner was within a few hundred yards of the shore, the attack and subsequent panic caused the deaths of over 5,000 people, all the more tragic since it came from the hands of those who would have liberated them a few days later. At the conclusion of the war, the burned-out hulk was broken up on the spot.

Holland–America Line

Statendam

Builders Harland & Wolff, Belfast, 1929
Specifications 29,511 gross tons; 697 ft (212 m) long, 81 ft (25 m) wide
Machinery Steam turbines; twin screw; speed 19 knots
Passengers 510 first class, 344 second class, 374 tourist class, 426 third class
Demise Destroyed in 1940

Queen of the spotless fleet from 1929 to 1938 was Statendam *(R. Scozzafava/Richard Morse Collection).*

At the conclusion of the First World War, Holland-America Line found itself short of tonnage for its New York route. *Potsdam* had been sold in 1915, it had lost the *Statendam/Justicia*, and its two 12,000-ton steamers *Nieuw Amsterdam* and *Rotterdam* were twenty years old. Accordingly, a new ship similar to the original *Statendam* was ordered from Harland & Wolff.

The new *Statendam* was laid down in 1921, but owing to US immigration restrictions that resulted in a slump in transatlantic traffic, construction was slowed down. The liner was finally launched on 11 September 1924, but work was then suspended entirely until 1927 when the

Netherlands Government intervened. Although it was then possible to resume work, strikes by Belfast shipyard workers delayed the liner so much that eventually she was towed to Wilton's Slipway & Engineering Company at Rotterdam on 13 April 1927 for completion.

Holland America's new flagship was finally completed in March 1929, her building having occupied eight years, a record for a major North Atlantic liner. *Statendam* sailed on her maiden voyage from Rotterdam to New York on 11 April 1929 at a time when production in the United States had reached an all-time high. Prosperity seemed endless and profits secure as *Statendam* settled down to become affectionately known as the 'Queen of the Spotless Fleet'.

Seven decks were devoted to first class accommodation and public rooms. Starting on Sun Deck forward was a beautiful Palm Court with windows on three sides. Below on Promenade Deck was a range of public rooms. First was the Reading and Writing Room, followed by an entrance and then a Lounge where passengers could enjoy a game of cards, dancing or conversation. Passing through another entrance, passengers entered the Smoke Room decorated to provide a club-like atmosphere. Finally, there was the Verandah Café, and an enclosed promenade encircled these public rooms. A-Deck and B-Deck were devoted to cabins, C-Deck a double-decked dining-room, E-Deck additional cabins and F-Deck an indoor swimming-pool. A company brochure stated 'Her passenger accommodations have been designed with a view to real comfort combining the qualities of a luxurious hotel with those of a modern ship fitted to sail the seven seas', and how true it was for first class. The other classes were naturally less spacious.

The good times came to an abrupt end on Tuesday, 29 October 1929. Like all steamship companies, Holland-America then had to search for passengers. To entice the few that were there, HAL reclassified *Statendam's* accommodation in October 1931 to first, tourist and third. To cut down on port charges, her new weight in 1933 was 28,291 gross tons, not a significant decrease, but every penny counted during those harsh economic times. Her accommodation was reclassified again in May 1936 to cabin, tourist and third; the change from first to cabin was because of the new Cunard steamer *Queen Mary*. In addition to her regular transatlantic sailings, *Statendam* undertook a few cruises from New York during the slack winter seasons.

Despite the outbreak of war on the continent, *Statendam* continued to ply the Atlantic. However, when the Germans started to torpedo ships indiscriminately, Holland-America decided the risk was not worth it. *Statendam* departed from Rotterdam on what would be her last sailing on 24 November 1939; on her return to Rotterdam she was laid up.

The Second World War came to Holland on 10 May 1940 at 3.30 am, when German parachute troops floated down around Rotterdam and the city was heavily bombed. Caught in the artillery fire the next day was *Statendam*. She burned for three days beneath a pall of thick smoke, then, completely burned out, she was towed to Hendrik Ido Ambacht and scrapped in August 1940.

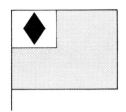

Inman Steamship Company

City of Rome

Builders Barrow Shipbuilding Company, Barrow, 1881
Specifications 8,415 gross tons; 586 ft (179 m) long, 52 ft (16 m) wide
Machinery Compound engines; single screw; speed 16 knots
Passengers 271 first class, 250 second class, 810 third class
Demise Scrapped in 1902

Considered by many to be one of the most stately and well-proportioned steamships ever built, *City of Rome* was designed by William John and intended to accomplish one task—to capture the westbound Blue Riband from White Star's *Germanic* and the eastbound from Guion's *Arizona*. *City of Rome* took to the water on 14 June 1881, and was completed four months later.

Sitting at her wharf at Liverpool, *City of Rome* was like a greyhound straining at the gate to show her mettle. Her clipper bow was adorned with the figurehead of Emperor Hadrian and her stern, embossed in gold, glittered with the arms and crest of the Eternal City. Her trio of closely-spaced white-banded funnels emanated power, while her four pole masts, of which the first three were fitted with yards for auxiliary sails, pointed skyward at an angle.

City of Rome had exquisitely appointed interiors. Her music-room was panelled in ebony and gold. The grand saloon was dressed in neutral hues and pastel tapestries, and lit by a 20 ft long oval skylight. Equally sumptuous was the ladies' boudoir. It had walls of brocaded silk, a ceiling of Japanese leather paper, chairs and couches upholstered in blue velvet and window hangings of Roman cloth with banded stripes of plush. Finally, for the gentlemen, the smoking-room, with its dark panellings and mohair coverings with seats upholstered in pigskin was a perfect retreat. Illumination of the public rooms and engine spaces was by electricity.

On 13 October 1881, Inman's flagship departed from Liverpool on her maiden voyage to New York, with passengers paying £20 ($100) for first cabin, £16 ($80) for second cabin and £6 ($28) for steerage accomodation. Expectations were high as she sailed down the Mersey to the open sea, but it took her 9 days 17 hours to complete the passage from Queenstown to New York, far longer than *Germanic's* 7½-day record passage. Homeward, the voyage occupied 8 days 7 hours 45 minutes, 25 hours more than *Arizona's*.

She had clearly disappointed her owners. Inman cancelled her winter schedule and handed her back to Barrow for a complete engine overhaul and the fitting of a new propeller. She re-emerged in April and commenced her second voyage on 6 April 1882. Both passages were an improvement, under 8 days, but still too slow for the Riband. *City of Rome* undertook four additional voyages from Liverpool before being handed over to Anchor Line in August 1882. In addition to her disappointing performance was

Above *The first three-funnel ever built,* City of Rome (Princeton University, SSHSA Collection).

Below *Externally,* City of Rome *is believed by many to be the most beautiful ship ever built* (SSHSA Collection).

her limited freight capacity of 2,200 tons instead of the 3,800 tons stipulated in the building contract, the difference being accounted for by the substitution of iron for steel; at the time of construction the latter was in short supply.

City of Rome immediately became Anchor Line's flagship and the largest vessel it owned until the advent of *Columbia* in 1902. She commenced her first voyage under the Anchor Line house-flag on 25 August 1882, and made 58 round trips from Liverpool to New York via Queenstown. On 7 May 1891, she was refitted to carry 75 first class, 250 second class and 1,000 steerage passengers from Glasgow and Moville (Ireland) to New York. In September 1898, she participated in the end of the Spanish–American War by repatriating 1,690 Spanish officers and men from Portsmouth to Santander.

At the turn of the century, Anchor Line gave careful consideration to bringing *City of Rome* up to date by re-engining her, but the cost proved prohibitive. It was therefore decided to retire the graceful lady. On 26 September 1901, *City of Rome* commenced her last voyage from Glasgow. Three months later, on 12 December, she left New York empty for Glasgow and was laid up; the following year she was scrapped in Germany.

Though she failed to please her first owners, *City of Rome* did set a pattern for the lavish interior appointments to be expected of a flagship. Inman wanted to forget her mechanical failings, but repeated her exterior lines and improved on her interiors in their future liners, *City of New York* and *City of Paris*.

Inman & International Steamship Company

City of New York

Builders J. & G. Thomson, Glasgow, 1888
Specifications 10,499 gross tons; 560 ft (170 m) long, 63 ft (19 m) wide
Machinery Triple expansion engines; twin screw; speed 20 knots
Passengers 540 first class, 200 second class, 1,000 steerage
Demise Scrapped in 1923

Inman Line was reorganized in 1886 as the Inman & International Steamship Company. Although I & I was a subsidiary of International Navigation Company, an American controlled and financed shipping conglomerate, Inman ships continued to fly the British flag. In 1887, Inman placed an order with J. & G. Thomson for a pair of large, fast liners that would eclipse anything afloat. Thomson fulfilled Inman's request, and the results were the creation of what many people considered the most beautiful liners to ply the North Atlantic, *City of New York* and *City of Paris*.

The first to be completed was *City of New York*. Launched on 15 March 1888, she was completed in July and sent on her maiden voyage from Liverpool to New York on 1 August 1888.

City of New York and her sister provided a superb example of the skill and craftmanship of Clydeside shipbuilding. With their figureheads, clipper stems and short bowsprits, the long sweeping lines of their black hulls, three closely-spaced black funnels, three pole masts and ornate, rounded sterns, they presented an unforgettable sight. For a short period of time, both ships' foremasts were fitted with yards for the carriage of sails.

The two 'Cities' had many technical innovations—they were the first 'express' liners on the North Atlantic propelled by twin screws, their machinery installation comprised two sets of triple expansion engines, 'water chambers' were installed in the hope that they would lessen rolling in heavy seas and each ship had 15 watertight compartments separated by strong transverse bulkheads rising from the keel to the saloon deck some 18 ft above the load water-line.

In addition to the safety features, Inman paid close attention to the interiors of its liners, with the result that both were lavishly furnished for the comfort of passengers. The first class staterooms were large and lofty and well ventilated by fans and patent ventilators. Each was provided with basins that had taps for hot and cold running water (a novel feature), a button to summon their steward instead of shouting down the corridor and, the most significant innovation, electric lights. Passengers were now able to take a nap or retire early by simply flicking a switch. Some cabins were convertible to sitting-rooms, and each ship had 14 suites large enough to entertain friends, complete with their own lavatory and bath.

First class passengers dined in a room located close to midships, decorated with naiads, dolphins, Tritons and mermaids. The arched roof of glass was 53 ft long and 25 ft wide and its height from floor to crown was 20 ft. Besides the long tables in the centre there were a number of small ones placed in alcoves. Seating was in bolted-down revolving armchairs, replacing the long, regimented benches. Socializing took place in the smoking-room, 45 ft long with its walls and ceiling panelled in black walnut and couches and chairs covered with scarlet leather, the drawing-room or the library, with its 900 volumes, oak wainscotting and stained glass windows inscribed with quotations from poems referring to the sea. Provision was also made in the dining-room to observe the Sabbath; at each end of the saloon was an oriel window built under the glass dome, and the casement of one of these served for a pulpit and the opposite one contained an organ.

Second class passengers were placed aft and allocated a dining-room, smoking-room, a piano

American Line's New York *heading for Europe* (Everett E. Viez, SSHSA Collection).

and a little deck space. According to a contemporary account, steerage was given a generous '300,000 cubic feet of space'.

Once *City of New York* settled down, she managed to capture the Blue Riband in August 1892, when she covered the 2,814 miles from Sandy Hook to Queenstown in 5 days 19 hours 57 minutes, averaging 20.11 knots during the voyage. She thus became the first ship to reduce the eastbound Atlantic passage to less than six days. Nine months later, however, Cunard's *Campania* relieved *City of New York* of this distinction.

After years of negotiations between I & I and the United States Postmaster-General, *City of New York* and *City of Paris*, under an act authorized by Congress, were transferred to American registry on 10 May 1892 and placed under the banner of International Navigation Company (American Line). Four months later it was announced that the Postmaster-General had accepted American Line's tender to carry the American mails between New York and South-

New York *with only two funnels following her 1901 refit*
(R. Loren Graham, SSHSA Collection).

ampton. Before sailing for her new owners, *City of New York* was given a refit that saw her passenger capacity reduced to 290 first class, 250 second class and 725 third class passengers, and her tonnage increased to 10,508.

In an elaborate ceremony on 22 February 1893 in New York harbour that included President Harrison, members of his cabinet, Congressmen, Senators, prominent officials and thousands of patriotic citizens witnessing the event at Battery Park, *City of New York* was officially handed over to American Line and renamed *New York*, the President performing the honours. His last remarks were, 'I deem it an entirely appropriate function that the President of the United States should lift the flag'. He then seized the ensign halyards, and as the bundle of silk slowly mounted the staff there was a flash of blue and white, then a blaze of crimson—'Old Glory' was proudly flying over the stern. Wild cheers from the excited citizens and thunderous salutes from harbour craft followed.

Three days after the celebration, *New York* departed for Southampton. Her beautiful first

class appointments were kept, and her second cabin and third class were improved. American Line described the second cabin dining saloon as 'a handsome and well lighted apartment 45 ft long and 40 ft wide providing seats for 250 passengers'. It also contained a piano. There was a smoking-room, a well-stocked library, a Ladies' Room and the after part of the Promenade Deck for their exclusive use. For third class, gone were the large dormitories and in their place were two, four and six berth cabins. The berths were metal and were fitted with woven wire-sprung bases. Each section of third class had a pantry which furnished hot water for coffee or tea. The most important improvement was the dining-room. Finished in white, the apartment had permanent tables and revolving chairs, a feature normally limited to first and second class. The tables were covered with cloths and a number of stewards waited upon the diners and cared for the eating utensils. Finally, the chamber had a piano, thus 'offering every facility for all kinds of entertainments and amusements'. Naturally reference was made to the electric lighting, steam heating and proper ventilation for all classes.

In 1898, *New York* was chartered to the United States Government and handed over to the Navy, for whom she sailed as the auxiliary cruiser *Harvard* during the Spanish-American War. When the conflict concluded, her name reverted to *New York* and she returned to her former route.

With the great advances being made in engineering, and newer, larger and faster competition coming into service, American Line decided to re-engine *New York*. She was taken the the William Cramp shipyard at Philadelphia in May

1901 and fitted with new triple expansion engines. In the process, her middle funnel was removed and her tonnage was listed at 10,798. She returned to the New York-Cherbourg-Southampton run in April 1903, but at 25 years old she could not compete for first class passengers with the likes of *Mauretania, Olympic* and *Imperator,* so American Line simply renamed her first class accomodation second class.

With the outbreak of war in Europe, *New York* was switched in August 1914 to Liverpool. She sailed from there until requisitioned by the US Government in 1917 when she was again turned over to the Navy, renamed *Plattsburg* and em-

New York *as the troop transport USS* Plattsburg (National Archives, Washington DC).

ployed as an armed troop transport, minus her second mast. Returned to American Line in 1919, the ageing liner reverted to her original name and once again plied between New York and Southampton from 19 February 1920. American Line finally retired this graceful but now tired queen in November 1920.

The Polish Navigation Company, an American firm established in 1921, purchased *New York* and she departed from New York for Antwerp, Danzig and Southampton on 14 September 1921. Accomodation was provided for 600 cabin class and 1,000 third class passengers. At the last port, the liner was detained for lack of credit to obtain supplies—coal, fresh water and provisions. On 12 October *New York* left Southampton with half-empty bunkers for Cherbourg where a Company agent told the captain to sail to Brest where his coal bunkers would be filled. *New York* finally puffed into New York on 30 October with 17 cabin and 38 third class passengers, and, since Polish Navigation failed to please their creditors, she was promptly seized by US Marshalls.

Placed on the selling block, the ageing vessel was sold in 1922 to Worden & Company of New York. She was quickly resold to Irish American Line whose intention was to start a passenger service betwen New York and Ireland, but that came to nothing. *New York* was then acquired in 1922 by United Transatlantic Line, an American company.

United chartered *New York* to American Black Sea Line, under whose house-flag the ship departed from New York on 19 June 1922, with 71 first class, 265 second class and 598 steerage passengers for Naples and Constantinople. At Constantinople, she was sold by auction on the instructions of the US Government. After 34 years of faithful service *New York* arrived in Genoa in 1923 to be scrapped.

City of Paris

(Paris, Yale, Philadelphia, Harrisburg)

Builders J. & G. Thomson, Glasgow, 1889
Specifications 10,499 gross tons; 560 ft (170 m) long, 63 ft (19 m) wide
Machinery Triple expansion engines; twin screw; speed 20 knots
Passengers 540 first class, 200 second class, 1,000 steerage
Demise Scrapped in 1923

City of Paris *at her wharf* (Princeton University, SSHSA Collection).

City of Paris was the second of a pair of express liners ordered by Inman in 1887. She made her debut on the Atlantic when she departed from Liverpool on 3 April 1889. Within a month she had established herself as a speed queen and in May 1889 she snatched the Blue Riband from Cunard's *Etruria* by steaming from Queenstown to Sandy Hook in 5 days 23 hours 7 minutes at an average speed of 19.95 knots, the first ship to make the westbound crossing in less than six days. Eastbound, departing from New York on 15 May, she covered the 2,894 miles in 6 days 29 minutes at an average speed of 20.03 knots; sister ship *City of New York* broke the eastbound six day barrier in August 1892. White Star's crack steamers *Majestic* and *Teutonic* wrested the westbound Riband from *City of Paris* in 1891, but she regained it in 1892, only to lose it permanently in 1893 to Cunard's *Campania*.

The exterior and interior of *City of Paris* were similar to that of her sister ship *City of New York*, under both I & I and American Line banners. Therefore, to avoid repetition of superlatives, suffice it to say that *City of Paris* was the faster of the two.

During an eastbound voyage in March 1890, the starboard propellor shaft broke at high speed. The racing engine completely wrecked itself and caused a leak that turned into a flood, putting the port engine also out of action. The ship was towed to Queenstown to be repaired, resuming operations in May 1891.

City of Paris was part of the acquisition completed on 10 May 1892 between I & I and the United States Postmaster-General by an Act of Congress. Delivery date was set for February 1893, and *City of Paris* was refitted to carry 290 first class, 250 second class and 725 third class passengers. Under United States registry at 10,508 tons and her name shortened to *Paris*, the graceful liner departed from New York under the American line banner on 25 March 1893 for Southampton.

Paris was chartered by the US Government in 1898 and turned over to the Navy. Given the name *Yale*, she operated as an auxiliary cruiser in the Spanish-American War. At the conclusion of hostilities, she was returned to American Line, her name reverted to *Paris* and she resumed transatlantic sailings on 10 October 1898 from New York.

Leaving Southampton on 21 May 1899 in heavy fog, *Paris* became stranded on the Manacles off Cornwall. Pierced and held fast by the notorious granite fangs, she lay there for seven

Tugs trying to free City of Paris *from the Manacles* (Wilfred Warren, SSHSA Collection).

American Line's Philadelphia (National Archives, Washington DC).

weeks. Finally, on 11 July, she was refloated by Liverpool Salvage Association, and, after temporary repairs in Falmouth and Milford Haven, was sent to Harland and Wolff, Belfast, for refitting. She was given new quadruple expansion engines, her tonnage was increased to 10,786 and her second funnel was removed. Now *Philadelphia*, she commenced her first voyage under her new name from Southampton to New York on 31 August 1901. In 1913, her first class accommodation was restyled second class.

Following the outbreak of the First World War, *Philadelphia* was switched to Liverpool, and in 1917 was taken over by the US Government, handed to the Navy and renamed *Harrisburg*; her second mast was removed. As an armed troop transport, she ferried American 'doughboys' to the European battlefields. When the conflict ended, she was returned to American Line in 1919 and her name reverted to *Philadelphia*. She set sail again from New York on 12 March 1920, but in

November the ageing liner and former speed queen was laid up.

A purchaser materialized in the form of the New York – Naples Steamship Company, an American company formed in 1922. Advertisements in the *New York Times* stated 'S.S. *Philadelphia* "Fast American Mail Steamer", first and second class accommodations calling at Gibraltar, Naples, Palermo, Piraeus, Constantinople sailing July 1'. The old lady was spruced up and on the appointed date, 1 July, *Philadelphia* backed out of her New York pier for the Mediterranean. *En route,* a mutiny broke out among the crew, and officers had to patrol the ship with loaded revolvers. An attempt was made to scuttle her and fire broke out. The ageing dowager sailed into Naples, where she was beached to prevent her from sinking. She then suffered further indignities when the Italian Government sequestered her for bad debts. The American Consul provided funds to repatriate the crew to the States, but the ship remained in Naples until she was purchased by the scrappers at Genoa, whence she was towed in 1923 to join her sister, *New York*.

International Navigation Company

Belgenland

(Belgic, Columbia)

Builders Harland & Wolff, Belfast, 1917
Specifications 27,132 gross tons; 697 ft (212 m) long, 78 ft (24 m) wide
Machinery Triple expansion engines and steam turbines; triple screw; speed 17 knots
Passengers 500 first class, 500 second class, 1,500 third class
Demise Scrapped in 1936

International Navigation Company Limited was a British concern and member of Morgan's International Mercantile Marine Company, a conglomerate founded to consolidate and control transatlantic shipping. Though *Belgenland* was owned by International Navigation, her marketing agent and funnel colours were that of Red Star, a Belgian line and another member of IMM.

International's flagship Belgenland *passing Morro Castle* (Everett E. Viez, SSHSA Collection).

Belgenland was launched in 1914 for Red Star, but was completed in 1917 as the two-funnel, three-mast troopship and cargo steamer *Belgic* for White Star. After the Armistice in 1918, *Belgic* made a few voyages between Liverpool and New York until 1921 when she returned to Harland and Wolff for an extensive overhaul that included conversion to oil-fired engines and additions to her passenger accommodation. These alterations increased her tonnage from 24,547 to 27,132. In addition, her two funnels were now three and her masts reduced from three to two, and, once handed over to International Navigation, her name reverted to *Belgenland*. Under British registry, but flying the Red Star banner, *Belgenland* departed from Antwerp for Southampton and New York on 4 April 1923. In January 1924, she left New York on a world cruise, an event she undertook every winter. Among her unique features for these cruises were three swimming-pools, two out-

doors and one down below inside.

Changing US immigration laws and a new kind of sophisticated eastbound traveller dictated the rearrangement of her accommodation. In April 1927, the worst of second class and the best of third class were designated as a new class known as tourist third cabin. In May 1929, second class was eliminated and the accommodation became first, tourist and third. As the October 1929 Depression made itself felt worldwide, *Belgenland* began to spend more and more time on short cruises. In 1932, she spent the greater part of the year laid up in Antwerp. During the summer of 1933 she made three Mediterranean cruises from London, then was laid up there.

With Red Star in rapid decline, *Belgenland* was transferred to the American firm of Panama

Belgic *sailed as a two-funnel liner between 1917 and 1921* (Henry W. Uhle, SSHSA Collection).

Panama Pacific's flagship Columbia *leaves New York on another cruise* (Everett E. Viez, SSHSA Collection).

Pacific Line. She departed from London on 10 January 1935, in ballast for New York. Upon arrival she was renamed *Columbia*, registered in the United States at 24,578 tons and painted white. *Columbia's* first voyage was a Nassau, Miami and Havana cruise that departed from New York on 16 February 1935. Her regular run commenced in March 1935 between New York and San Franciso via the Panama Canal.

Columbia proved, however, to be unprofitable on the intercoastal run, as well as on 13-day Caribbean cruises that started at $145 (£30). She was therefore laid up during the latter part of 1935 and offered for sale. A purchaser, P. & W. McLellan, arrived and relieved Panama Pacific of their burden. Placed once more under the British flag, she left New York on 22 April 1936 for Bo'ness, Scotland, to be broken up.

Messageries Maritimes

Champollion

Builders Construction Navales, La Ciotat, 1925
Specifications 12,263 gross tons; 520 ft (158 m) long, 62 ft (19 m) wide
Machinery Triple expansion engine; twin screw; speed 15 knots
Passengers 188 first class, 133 second class, 128 third class, 500 steerage
Demise Wrecked in 1952

Champollion *sporting her new Maierform bow* (Richard Morse Collection).

Champollion was completed in 1925 and on 14 September she was dispatched on Messageries Maritimes' Marseille-Alexandria service. After eight years *Champollion* was taken into La Ciotat in November 1933 for rebuilding, as the owners were no longer satisfied with her performance. Her tonnage was increased to 12,644 tons by the installation of additional low pressure turbines and a new Maierform forepart that increased her length to 550 ft (167 m). Returned to service in 1934, she was now able to dash across the Mediterranean at 17.5 knots.

After the fall of France in 1940, *Champollion* was laid up at Algiers. In December 1942, she

The more streamlined Champollion *after the war* (Compagnie Générale Maritime).

was taken over by the Allies and served as a troop transport. After VE day and reparations work, *Champollion* was handed back to Messageries Maritimes in 1946. The company immediately pressed her into Far East service ferrying civil servants and troops between Marseille and French Indochina. Once France began to re-assert her control in Asia, Messageries Maritimes took *Champollion* to La Ciotat for a much needed refit. The work started in September 1950, and when *Champollion* emerged in March 1951 and re-entered the Marseille-Alexandria service, her three funnels were reduced to one, her tonnage was decreased to 12,546 and her passengers were given a little more room. Her new capacity was 207 first class, 142 second class and 150 third class passengers.

In the early hours of 22 December 1952, *Champollion* was approaching Beirut in very bad weather. By mistake, the ship's navigators had set a course based on an airport beacon which happened to be operating that night. As a result, the ship ran aground on Elchat Elmahoun reef, three miles south of the port. Buffeted by heavy breakers and a stiff westerly wind the stranded liner slowly cracked amidships with the terrified passengers still on board. Each successive wave enlarged the fissure, and two attempts by the crew to reach shore in their lifeboats failed, as one capsized and another was swamped. By the afternoon of the following day, 313 persons had been rescued by harbour and naval craft, but fifteen died in an attempt to swim to shore. During the night, *Champollion* broke in two on the sand bar, and the wreck was sold to a Lebanese firm for scrapping.

Mariette Pacha

Builders Constructions Navales, La Ciotat, 1925
Specifications 12,239 gross tons; 520 ft (158 m) long, 62 ft (19 m) wide
Machinery Triple expansion engines; twin screw; speed 15 knots
Passengers 188 first class, 133 second class, 128 third class, 500 steerage
Demise Sunk in 1944

Mariette Pacha was *Champillion's* sister ship ordered by Messageries Maritimes from La Ciotat, and she joined her sister on the Marseille-

Though a bit crowded in steerage, Mariette Pacha *plies on. Note the wind scoops by each porthole to catch a little breeze (Compagnie Générale Maritime).*

Alexandria service in October 1925. Unlike *Champollion,* however, Messageries Maritimes decided not to put money into refitting *Marietta Pacha,* so she continued in service in her original condition until she was laid up at Marseille in 1940.

During the evacuation of France in August 1944, *Mariette Pacha* was scuttled by the retreating German troops. The wreck was raised and broken up in 1946.

Norddeutscher Lloyd

Spree

(Kaiserin Maria Theresia, Ural)

Builders Vulcan A. G, Stettin, 1890
Specifications 6,963 gross tons; 463 ft (141 m) long (bp), 51 ft (16 m) wide
Machinery Triple expansion engines; single screw; speed 18 knots
Passengers 244 first class, 122 second class, 460 steerage
Demise Sunk in 1905

Spree was the second ship built at a German yard for North German Lloyd (NDL). The first was *Kaiser Wilhelm II* in 1889, and the third was *Havel* in 1891, all three originally having three masts and only two funnels. *Spree* and *Havel* were constructed as sister ships for NDL's express service between Bremen and New York.

Completed in September 1890, *Spree* com-

Spree in her original two-funnel form (Alex Shaw, SSHSA Collection).

Kaiserin Maria Theresia *at the dockside* (Hapag-Lloyd AG).

menced her maiden voyage on 11 October, and by August 1891 NDL had no fewer than 12 express steamers operating between Bremen and New York on a bi-weekly basis. However, *Spree* and *Havel* failed to cause a sensation, being slightly smaller and slower than HAPAG'S quartet of *Augusta Victoria, Columbia, Normannia* and *Furst Bismarck,* introduced at the same time. Also, *Spree* had her difficulties. On 26 November 1892, she fractured her propeller shaft and had to be towed to Queenstown by *Lake Huron*. It fractured again on 2 July 1897, and three days later the drifting *Spree* was sighted by *Maine,* who hooked a line aboard and towed her to Queenstown. At the end of the 1897 season, she was withdrawn from service; single screw express steamers were fast becoming obsolete.

In 1899, *Spree* was taken into Vulcan for some work. Out went the triple expansion, five cylinder engine and in its place a new triple expansion, eight cylinder engine was installed. Twin propellers were fitted, the fore area lengthened by 65 ft (20 m), the second mast removed, a third funnel added and her passenger accommodation altered. To complete the refit, NDL renamed her *Kaiserin Maria Theresia.*

When *Kaiserin Maria Theresia* made her debut in March 1900, she was practically a new ship—two masts, three funnels, 7,840 gross tons, 528 ft (170 m) long, propelled by twin screws and carrying 405 first class, 114 second class and 387 steerage passengers. 'KMT' served as a reserved ship on the Bremen-New York run and on the Mediterranean-New York route, making seven round trips; at other times she was employed as a cruise ship.

In 1904, *Kaiserin Maria Theresia* was sold to the Russians and became *Ural,* a Russian auxiliary cruiser. She served in the Pacific in the Russo-Japanese War of 1905, only to be sunk on 27 May 1905 at the Battle of Tsushima.

Kaiser Friedrich
(Burdigala)

Builders F. Schichau, Danzig, 1898
Specifications 12,481 gross tons; 600 ft (183 m) long, 64 ft (19 m) wide

Machinery Quadruple expansion engines; twin screw; speed 19 knots
Passengers 400 first class, 250 second class, 700 steerage
Demise Sunk in 1916

North German Lloyd (NDL) had two objectives in the mid-1890s. The first was to put an end to the dominance of Cunard's *Campania* and *Lucania* by building the fastest ship in the world, and the second was to gain the patronage of British and American passengers while in the process of gaining the Blue Riband. NDL presented its plans to Germany's shipyards with one stipulation—build us the fastest ship in the world and we'll buy it. Vulcan accepted the challenge and in 1897 came up with a winner, the four-funnel *Kaiser Wilhelm der Grosse*. She snatched the Blue Riband in September by steaming at an average of 22.27 knots. The *crème de la crème* flocked to NDL and their new liner.

F. Schichau of Danzig was awarded another contract to produce a second would-be record-breaker on the same basis. North German Lloyd's rival, Hamburg-America, as well as the

North German Lloyd's bubble burst after Kaiser Friedrich*'s disappointing maiden voyage* (Everett E. Viez, SSHSA Collection).

premier North Atlantic companies Cunard, White Star and American Line, nervously awaited this new vessel. Another *Kaiser Wilhelm der Grosse,* and they could say farewell to their first class traffic!

Launched by Schichau on 5 October 1897, *Kaiser Friedrich* was completed in May 1898. During trials, however, she scarcely managed 20 knots, which was short of the required 22 knots. NDL thus refused to accept her, but Schichau guaranteed that they would put the matter right, on the strength of which the ship was put provisionally into service. Hoping for the best, NDL dressed up their second largest ship in flags, and sailed her from Bremen on 7 June 1898, under the command of Captain L. A. Stormen. After a call at Southampton, she arrived in New York 7 days 11 hours later with her 392 passengers. Her return took a disappointing 9 days 2 hours 30 minutes. Deemed unacceptable, NDL cancelled her second and third voyages and returned her to Schichau for some engine work and to be lightened. The competition was relieved.

Trials commenced again in September 1898 with a slight improvement in performance. *Kaiser Friedrich* then resumed her transatlantic sailings, completing three round trips at the end of that year. During those voyages, first class pas-

Kaiser Friedrich coaling at Pier 1, Hoboken, New Jersey, in 1898 (Albert E. Gayer, SSHSA Collection).

sengers enjoyed the use of a dining salon surmounted by a large, light 'well' extended upwards to the Promenade Deck, where it occupied the centre of the lounge and smoking-room. All first and second class cabins were located as high up in the ship as possible to increase safety and comfort, and a number of first class cabins could be converted into sitting-rooms.

During the winter of 1899, NDL sent the liner back to Schichau for further reconstructions, including the lengthening of each funnel by 14 ft 6 in. She underwent more trials, then went back on the Atlantic ferry run on 5 March 1899. Her best passage was a westbound trip of 6 days 22 hours 30 minutes. Unfortunately she could not manage more than 20 knots, making her an unsuitable running mate for the speedy *Kaiser Wilhelm der Grosse*. Totally disillusioned with these poor performances, NDL finally returned *Kaiser Friedrich* to her builder in June 1899.

The proud firm of F. Schichau told NDL that it could not give back *Kaiser Friedrich* since she had never been officially accepted in the first place. Schichau's management said that *they* would withdraw her from service and dispose of the ship in their own way. The affair became an international scandal lasting years, and payment for the vessel was eventually settled out of court.

In the meanwhile, *Kaiser Friedrich* was laid up at Hamburg until chartered by Hamburg-America in October 1899. She commenced sailing on HAPAG's 'express' Hamburg–Southampton–Cherbourg–New York service on the first of that month and in all made ten round trips, the last departing from Hamburg on 11 October 1900. Upon arrival she was laid up, and rested at her moorings in the harbour of Hamburg for twelve long years, the biggest 'white elephant' since *Great Eastern*.

Kaiser Friedrich was rescued from this state by the newly-formed Compagnie de Navigation Sud Atlantique, which had been awarded a mail contract between Bordeaux and South America. Sud Atlantique had ordered two ships, *Lutetia* and *Gallia,* on 1 January 1912 for this service, but in the meantime it needed a big ship to fill the gap until the arrival of the new ships in 1913. Therefore, on 1 May 1912, it bought *Kaiser Friedrich* for £165,000 ($800,000). She was taken into Blohm & Voss for refitting and the installation of new boilers.

She emerged from Blohm & Voss as *Burdigala* (the Roman name for Bordeaux) with a white

Above Kaiser Friedrich *laid up in the backwaters of Hamburg* (Hapag-Lloyd AG).

Below Sud Atlantique's *flagship and 'speed queen'*, Burdigala (Henry W. Uhle, SSHSA Collection).

hull (later, on second thoughts, painted black). With a red cockerel affixed to each side of her black-topped buff funnels, *Burdigala* finally set sail from Bordeaux on 5 October 1912 (she was supposed to sail in September) as the largest and nominally the fastest ship on the southern route. Within weeks she was in trouble, and was unable to depart on her second voyage on time; Sud Atlantique had to charter *La Gascogne* to fill the void. After repairs, *Burdigala* was returned to service in December. Once *Lutetia* and *Gallia* were delivered in November 1913, Sud Atlantique was only too pleased to get rid of *Burdigala*, and she was promptly laid up.

Short of tonnage, the French Navy requisitioned her in March 1915 and converted her into a transport carrying troops to the Dardanelles and Salonica. In December she was commissioned as a merchant cruiser with an armament of four 5.5 in guns.

Burdigala sailed from Salonica on 13 November 1916 with Lieutenant-Commander Rolland in command. At 10.45 the next morning, two miles south-west of St Nicolo in the Aegean, she was rocked by an explosion. It was a mine laid by German U-boat *U-73*. The sea flooded the engine and boiler rooms, Rolland gave the order to abandon ship and, 35 minutes after hitting the mine, *Burdigala* disappeared beneath the sea, a sad end for a sorry ship.

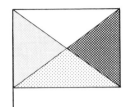

Peninsular & Oriental Steam Navigation Company

Naldera

Builders Caird & Company, Greenock, 1920
Specifications 15,825 gross tons; 605 ft (184 m) long, 67 ft (20 m) wide
Machinery Quadruple expansion engines; twin screw; speed 17 knots
Passengers 426 first class, 247 second class
Demise Scrapped in 1938

In 1913, P & O ordered a pair of liners for their Australian mail service. Both of the new ships were laid down in 1914, but work was halted at

Naldera served as P & O's flagship for only 14 days (P & O Group).

the outbreak of the First World War. In 1917, the Government took over their construction and authorized their completion, since the slipways were urgently needed for warship construction. *Naldera* was launched on 29 December 1917, and *Narkunda* followed on 25 April 1918.

Naldera was completed in 1918 as a troop-ship, but not before other ideas—conversion to a two-funnel armed merchant cruiser, fast cargo ship, hospital ship and aircraft carrier—had been put forward by the Government. In the event, the Armistice was signed before *Naldera* could set sail in grey; she and *Narkunda* were handed back to P & O in 1918 and the liners were completed according to the original plans.

The P & O directors felt that three funnels were a symbol of size and power and so had

Naldera and *Narkunda* fitted with them—the first and third were dummies. In addition, the twins were given cruiser sterns, and were the last P & O ships to have coal-fired boilers in preference to the geared turbines and oil firing favoured by companies building new ships after the war. Each ship had a bunker capacity for 1,895 tons of coal, of which 200 tons were burned each day at a speed of 17.5 knots. *Naldera* was distinguishable from *Narkunda* by her slightly raised forecastle, her 'old ivory' saloon decorations that inartistic passengers thought were dirty white, and her white superstructure. Later the superstructure was painted in the light-stone colour carried by the rest of the P & O fleet.

Naldera was completed in March 1920, and set sail for Australia as P & O's flagship on 10 April. The distinct honour of flagship lasted for only 14 days, then it was passed to *Narkunda*. Passage was from London via the Suez to Bombay, then south to Australia. In 1931, her route was switched to Bombay and the Far East, though

Naldera *looks 1,000 feet long in this early photograph* (P & O Group).

she did make one sailing to Sydney in June 1934.

Naldera was not one of P & O's lucky ships. On 29 July 1921, while departing from Bombay for Sydney, she collided with *Clan Lamont* and sustained damage to her bows. She put back into Bombay for repairs. On 2 October 1924, while docking at Tilbury, *Scotstoun Head* collided with her, causing some damage to the port side amidships; *Naldera* underwent repairs for two weeks. Homeward bound in July 1930, between Fremantle and Colombo, *Naldera* ran into severe gales that caused superstructure damage, and in October 1934, heading out to Bombay, she ran aground in the Suez Canal, but was refloated 24 hours later. Finally, on 16 January 1937, while docking at Southampton to embark passengers and cargo for Bombay, she damaged her starboard propeller, resulting in a delay of 36 hours.

Her final passenger sailing from London took place on 20 May 1938, when she departed for Japan. On returning to London on 23 September she was destined for the scrapyard. However, before heading north she was chartered by the British Government during the Munich Crisis of October 1938, and fitted out to carry the British

P & O's mail steamer Narkunda (P & O Group).

Legion Volunteer Police to supervise the plebiscite about to take place in Czechoslovakia. She sailed from England but on 10 October Hitler made a speech condemning the British and cancelling the plebiscite, so *Naldera* returned to port and shortly thereafter was sold to P. & W. McLellan of Glasgow. She departed Tilbury on 19 November 1938 to be broken up at Bo'ness.

Narkunda

Builders Harland & Wolff, Belfast, 1920
Specifications 16,118 gross tons; 606 ft (184 m) long, 70 ft (21 m) wide
Machinery Quadruple expansion engines; twin screw; speed 17 knots
Passengers 426 first class, 247 second class
Demise Sunk in 1942

Narkunda was laid down in 1914 as the sister ship of *Naldera,* but work ceased on their construction with the outbreak of the First World War. Building resumed in 1917 under Government control, and *Narkunda* was launched on 25 April 1918. The liner was then laid up in an unfinished state due to confusion over her intended deployment. Handed back to P & O in 1918, *Narkunda* was completed and made ready for her maiden voyage in April 1920 as P & O's largest ship,

their first at over 16,000 gross tons (she was surpassed in size in 1922 by *Moldavia).*

Her first voyage was a round trip to Bombay that departed from London on 24 April. Her first trip out to Australia left London on 9 July, calling at Suez, Bombay and Melbourne. P & O's mail steamers did not cater for third class passengers, and *Narkunda* and *Naldera* kept to that tradition. This practice ended with the changing social and economic times in 1930 when *Mongolia's* second class became third class.

By the early 'thirties *Narkunda* was sailing to the Far East as well as Australia. In 1927, in an effort to prolong her life, P & O had decided to convert her to an oil burner, and additional modernization followed in 1935 when her second class was converted into tourist class, and again in 1938 when her first class capacity was reduced from 426 to 350 passengers.

Narkunda continued to sail for P & O until 1939. Her last peacetime departure from London was on 23 June 1939, for Sydney. On this voyage, while entering Colombo harbour on 16 July, a build-up of gas from fermentation in the cargo caused a huge explosion that blew off the number six cargo hatch. Four crew members were killed and 23 injured. Three hundred and fifty tons of cargo were damaged and after

a two-day delay *Narkunda* resumed her voyage. She made three more round voyages, two to Shanghai via the Suez Canal and one to Hong Kong via Cape Town, before arriving back in England in October 1940.

Her next sailing was in November 1941, from Liverpool to Penang via Cape Town with fare-paying passengers and troops. Arriving back at Liverpool in April 1941, she was officially taken over as a troop transport. She then took part in troop landing exercises, followed by dry-docking, then, after a short voyage to Freetown, she sailed to the Far East in November 1941 where she helped in the evacuation of Singapore. On 30 July 1942 *Narkunda* left the Clyde for the Suez via Durban. On arrival at Durban, it was announced that she would repatriate British diplomats in exchange for Japanese diplomats. For the occasion, four huge Union Jacks were flown, the word 'Diplomats' was painted in letters ten feet high on each side and the ship was floodlit during the night. She arrived at Liverpool on 9 October, and three weeks later, on 1 November, left to participate in 'Operation Torch', the invasion of North Africa.

Narkunda disembarked troops and stores at Algiers and Bougie, Algeria, and was on her way home when, on 14 November between 5.00 and 5.30 pm off Bougie, she was bombed by aircraft, the explosions causing severe underwater damage. She took on a heavy list to port and began to sink stern first. The order was given to abandon ship; 31 crew members perished with her, but the survivors were rescued by HMS *Cadmus*, P & O's *Stratheden* and Orient Line's *Ormonde*.

Strathnaver

Builders Vickers-Armstrong Ltd, Barrow, 1931
Specifications 22,547 gross tons; 664 ft (202 m) long, 80 ft (24 m) wide
Machinery Turbo-electric engines; twin screws; speed 21 knots
Passengers 498 first class, 668 tourist class
Demise Scrapped in 1962

The early 'thirties were not the best times to introduce new tonnage but what P & O had was

becoming vintage, and to keep one step ahead of their arch rival, Orient Line, Lord Inchcape found it necessary to order two steamers from Vickers-Armstrong. The first down the slipways was *Strathnaver* on 5 February 1931, followed by her sister ship *Strathaird* on 18 July. P & O departed from the tradition of naming their ships after overseas places by adopting the 'Strath' nomenclature for their next five steamers. *Strathnaver's* name was taken from the first title of Lord Inchcape, being a valley to the north of Loch Naver in Sutherland.

The two ships set the style and standard for all future P & O mail steamers that would culminate in the commissioning of *Arcadia* and *Iberia* in 1954. *Strathnaver* and *Strathaird* were the first P & O liners to sport the new white colour scheme for the hull (although it had been tried in 1894 on *Caledonia*) and it was accented with a red waterline. Capitalizing on the success of *Naldera* and *Narkunda*, and realizing that the most profitable liners on the prestigious North Atlantic run were

three-funnel steamers, P & O decided to maintain the image. On the new twins only the second funnel was functional, while the first and third were added to alleviate the public prejudice against 'less powerful' single-funnel ships, especially the new generation of 'O' ships for Orient Line. Moreover, hopefully to secure more than their share of the Australian market, P & O built the 'Strath' twins without a second class. Their lowest grade was called tourist class, and they were able to provide better accommodation for the money.

Passengers were accommodated on seven decks. First class was allocated the forward portion of A, B, C, D and E decks. Public rooms were situated on B-Deck and consisted of a lounge, smoking-room, reading-room, writing-room, corridor lounge, verandah café, an open-air swimming-pool and a children's playroom. Staterooms were mostly single or double berth,

Strathnaver arriving at Sydney (P & O Group).

Strathnaver *leaving Sydney in 1940 with troops for the Middle East* (P & O Group).

many with private facilities. Tourist class had a smoking-room, lounge, children's nursery, verandah café and an outdoor swimming pool. Cabins accommodated two, four or six persons. Both dining-rooms were on F-Deck, separated by the galley, the 'Straths' were the first P & O ships to have running water in all passenger cabins.

Flags flying from stem to stern, *Strathnaver* hauled in her lines and departed from Tilbury on 1 October 1931 for Sydney and Brisbane via Marseille, Suez, Bombay and Colombo, the largest liner in the P & O fleet until the delivery of *Strathmore* in 1935. Except for a minor collision at the quay at Tilbury on 11 September 1937, *Strathnaver* spent her pre-war years on uneventful voyages to Australia and on periodic cruises from England and Australia. Most of her first class passengers southbound were top-ranking civil servants and commercial people while in tourist they were mostly migrants. Northbound came Australian families on four-month holidays visiting the family back in Britain or continental Europe.

At the end of a return journey to Sydney from Rabaul, New Britain (Papua New Guinea) *Strathnaver* was taken over by the Royal Navy on her arrival at Circular Quay, was painted grey and had two guns mounted on the poop. She sailed for Liverpool, arriving in October 1939, and was partially fitted out as a troop-ship. She then proceeded to Sydney where she embarked troops for the Middle East. For the duration of the war, she was sent trooping to South Africa, the Middle East and India under the management of the British government. She participated in the exercises in the Red Sea for the Italian landings, and twice during the war came under heavy air attack, escaping unscathed. She was retained by the government after the war to carry out repatriation work and it was under their

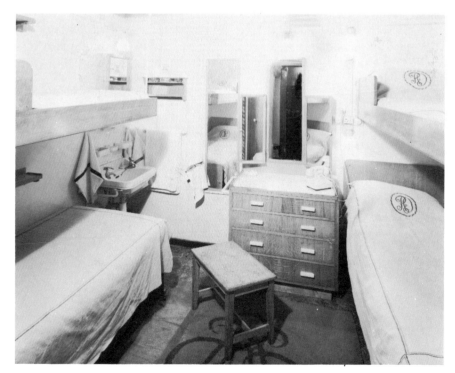

Above left Strathnaver's *funnels were reduced to one after the war* (P & O Group).

Left *The Dining Room aboard* Strathnaver *in a view taken after the war* (P & O Group).

Above *The first class lounge aboard* Strathnaver *after the war* (P & O Group).

Right *Compare* Strathnaver's *four-berth cabin with that of Cap Trafalgar in 1914 (page 125)* (P & O Group).

service that she rammed and sank the cargo ship *Fluor* on 10 October 1946.

Strathnaver was released from government service in 1948 and handed back to P & O. She was taken to Harland and Wolff and given a thorough refit that included the overhauling of the engines, reducing her cruising speed to 17.5 knots, the removal of the first and third dummy funnels to modernize her appearance, and the provision of accommodation for 573 first class and 496 tourist class passengers.

Registered at 22,270 gross tons, *Strathnaver* commenced her first post-war sailing from London on 5 January 1950, to Sydney. An honour was bestowed on *Strathnaver* on 15 June 1953, when she was chartered by the Government to take official guests around the fleet at the Coronation Fleet Review at Spithead.

With the withdrawal from service of the single-class steamers *Maloja* and *Mooltan,* and the introduction of *Arcadia* and *Iberia* in 1954, P & O decided to convert *Strathnaver* and *Strathaird* into single-class ships. In the former, space was made for 1,252 passengers.

Fierce competition from foreign operators such as Lloyd Triestino, Flotta Lauro, Codagar, Sitmar and Chandris, running air-conditioned ships for the Australia emigrant trade, slackened the demand for P & O's 'hot' tonnage. Furthermore, the Australian government altered the migrant contract that had favoured British emig-

rants so, faced with 'modern' competition and a migrant contract that now favoured the Mediterranean companies, P & O withdrew *Strathnaver* upon her arrival at Tilbury on 23 February 1962. She was sold to Shun Fung Ironworks in Hong Kong for £325,500; departing from London on 1 March, she arrived at the scrapyards on 31 March.

Strathaird

Builders Vickers-Armstrong Ltd, Barrow, 1932
Specifications 22,544 gross tons; 664 ft (202 m) long, 80 ft (24 m) wide
Machinery Turbo-electric engines; twin screw; speed 20 knots
Passengers 498 first class, 668 tourist class
Demise Scrapped in 1961

The second of the 'white sisters' was launched on 18 July 1931 by Lady Margaret Shaw, daughter of Lady Inchcape. The name *Strathaird* derived from the title of Sir William Mackinnon, the founder of British India Steam Navigation Company, and was taken from a headland on the Isle of Skye. *Strathaird* was completed in January 1931 and, like her sister, broke with P & O tradition by being given a white hull and super-

Strathaird on sea trials (P & O Group).

Strathaird arriving off Gravesend (P & O Group).

structure, yellow funnels and a red water-line.

She set sail from Tilbury on 12 February 1932 for the Antipodes via the Suez Canal and Bombay. She was propelled across the oceans by twin screws driven by two synchronous three-phase electric motors. This was the fairly new turbo-electric machinery, first tried successfully by P & O in *Viceroy of India* in 1929. *Strathnaver* was also fitted with the same machinery, but in both ships the choice was less than satisfactory, and future P & O mail ships reverted back to the traditional steam turbines.

The only blemish on *Strathaird's* pre-war record was when a passenger died of smallpox in Fremantle in March 1938 and first class passengers had to be placed in quarantine. A planned cruise to Fiji was cancelled as a result.

Besides operating line voyages to Australia and India, P & O also operated cruises. In fact, this British concern was one of the early pioneers of cruising, taking organized groups on line runs to the Mediterranean as early as 1843 and returning them to England on other P & O ships. By 1904, they were operating their first cruise-only vessel, *Vectis*. Hoping to capture the Australian market, P & O decided to introduce cruises from Sydney, and the first, a five-day trip to Norfolk Island, departed on 23 December 1932 in *Strathaird*. Subsequent cruises were offered in the 1930s at irregular intervals by both *Strathnaver* and *Strathaird*.

On 17 July 1939 *Strathaird* departed from Fremantle and arrived alongside Tilbury landing-stage on 18 August. She was taken over by the Royal Navy in September, stripped of her luxurious fittings, painted grey and recertified to carry as many as 5,000 troops. She made voyages to Australia, the Middle East, North America, South Africa and India both solo and in convoys. In 1940 she was at Brest to help in the evacuation of over 6,000 troops and civilians in the last days before the fall of France, and in March 1941 she was involved in a collision with *Stirling Castle* on a voyage from the Clyde to the Suez Canal that

Strathaird *arriving at Tilbury on her last voyage, 18 June 1961* (P & O Group).

had to be abandoned as a result.

At the close of hostilities and reparation work, *Strathaird* was handed back to P & O in 1946. Taken back to her builders at Barrow, she was given a complete overhaul, including the removal of the first and third dummy funnels. She emerged at 22,568 gross tons with space for 573 first class and 496 tourist class passengers.

P & O's second post-war sailing to Australia was undertaken by *Strathaird* when she resumed service from London on 22 January 1948. Passages were now slower due to her reduced cruising speed of 17.5 knots. During the ensuing years she was joined by newer members of the P & O fleet, and eventually, with the arrival of *Arcadia* and *Iberia* in 1954, she was downgraded to a tourist-class-only ship, catering for 1,242 passengers.

In 1960, P & O and Orient Line merged to form the giant shipping concern of P & O-Orient Line. They made an assessment of their tonnage and decided that the pre-war vessels would have to be disposed of; the first casualty was *Strathaird*. She was withdrawn from service upon her arrival in London on 18 June 1961, and her replacement was to be the giant superliner *Canberra*. Six days after her arrival, *Strathaird* departed for Shun Fung Ironworks at Hong Kong, to whom she had been sold for £382,500. She arrived at the scrapyard exactly one month later, where her steel was melted down and re-rolled to be used as reinforcing bars in skyscraper blocks and in the buildings at Kai-Tak airport.

Royal Holland Lloyd

Limburgia
(Reliance)

Builders Joh C. Tecklenborg AG, Geestemunde, 1915
Specifications 19,980 gross tons; 615 ft (187 m) long, 72 ft (22 m) wide
Machinery Triple expansion engines; triple screw; speed 16 knots

Passengers 315 first class, 301 second class, 850 third class
Demise Burned in 1938

The second of Ballin's South American trio (the others were *Admiral von Tirpitz* and *William*

Royal Holland Lloyd's twins, Brabantia *arriving and* Limburgia *departing* (The Mariners' Museum, Newport News, Virginia).

Above Reliance *in American Line colours* (Frank O. Braynard Collection).

Below Reliance *sailing under HAPAG's buff funnel colours* (Richard Morse Collection).

O'Swald) was launched on 10 February 1914 as *Johann Heinrich Burchard* and completed on 20 November 1915. In the midst of the war in 1916, *Johann Heinrich Burchard,* and her twin *William O'Swald,* were secretly sold to Koninklijke Hollandsche Lloyd (Royal Holland Lloyd) of Amsterdam to replace its torpedoed flagship, *Tubania.* The Allies refused to recognize the transaction, and after the war they demanded that both ships be surrendered. Royal Holland, however, was adamant about keeping the pair, naming them *Limburgia* and *Brabantia* respectively. On 3 February 1920, *Limburgia* departed from Bremerhaven in thick fog and was thus able to shake off a British destroyer waiting to prevent her sailing and transfer. She reached Amsterdam two days later.

Within two months, on 14 April, *Limburgia* departed from home port for South America. At the time of her commissioning, she was the largest ship on the South America run, only to be surpassed in September by her sister ship.

Royal Holland grossly overcommitted their capital for the two ships and the market proved unprofitable, so to conserve their financial resources while bowing to international pressure over the 'illegal' takeover of the vessels, Royal Holland sold the twins on 4 January 1922 to American Ship & Commerce Corporation. It in turn commissioned them as the *Reliance (Limburgia)* and *Resolute (Brabantia)* under the management of United American Lines (UAL) in January 1922.

After a modest refit, *Reliance* was re-assessed at 19,582 gross tons and catered for 290 first class, 320 second class and 400 third class passengers. With her funnels painted in the UAL colours of yellow with two narrow blue bands, *Reliance* left Hamburg on her first voyage on 3 May 1922 for Southampton, Cherbourg and New York; the schedules were in cooperation with Hamburg-America Line. To increase patronage and ensure profitablility, UAL felt it wise in 1923 to switch the registry of *Reliance* from the US to Panama in order to avoid the noose of American Prohibition laws. In this exchange of flags, her tonnage was also reduced to 16,798, along with a corresponding saving in port charges. During the winter months, UAL sent *Reliance* cruising; on 9 February 1924 she departed on a 75-day Mediterranean cruise.

Like *Vaterland,* the boiler uptakes of the first and second funnel were divided and carried down the sides of the superstructure, allowing an unrestricted vista through the principal public rooms. The third funnel was a dummy. Passenger accommodation was spread over six decks. Social activity was concentrated on Promenade Deck where a range of pleasantly-decorated public rooms were situated. There was the smoking-room panelled in mahogany and furnished with club chairs, a Social Hall finished in blue-grey, richly ornamented and hung with a number of splendid paintings and the Winter Garden with its lofty arched dome of coloured glass. In addition, there was a writing-room and library, a Ladies' Parlour and a verandah. Aft on the same deck was a permanent, tiled swimming-pool with a retractable glass dome, and close by a large gymnasium. The dining-room was two decks below and extended across the full width of the ship. The two-deck high chamber was decorated in shades of pearl and grey and softly illuminated by hundreds of concealed incandescent bulbs, adding a special aura to the dining atmosphere. Diners were serenaded by an orchestra that played from a balcony. For the gastronome, there was also a Grill Room. Passenger cabins, all with bedsteads, were located on all decks, and included four de luxe suites.

United American also took care of their other passengers. In *Reliance,* second class meant 'occupying accommodation of every comfort and convenience'. There was a 'large and elegantly appointed dining-room, handsomely furnished social hall and a most inviting smoking-room'. Second class staterooms were furnished with berths. Little was mentioned of crowded third class. However, for the benefit of all passengers there was a botanical garden, the 'hot house' on board where hundreds of plants, both tropical and semi-tropical, were grown to add to the charm of the public rooms and staterooms.

To soothe whatever fears the travelling public might have had, UAL stressed the safety features of their two new ships. According to company literature, they were of the 'latest approved designs', including transverse and longitudinal

watertight bulkheads, smoke bulkheads, wireless, a submarine signalling system and a steam and water fire extinguishing system; for the passengers' comfort, bilge keels helped to reduce rolling in heavy seas.

By the mid-1920s, Hamburg-America was well on the road to rebuilding its once shattered fleet, and the company was also encroaching more on UAL itineraries. It therefore came as no surprise during the spring of 1926 when Edward Harriman, President of UAL, announced that Hamburg-America were to acquire three of UAL's former ships. Also included in the deal was an exchange of stock. In the end, HAPAG succeeded in driving UAL from the oceans.

Reliance undertook her last sailing for UAL from Hamburg on 25 June 1925, and on 24 August 1926 she sailed from that port under the colours of HAPAG. The transfer to German registry increased her tonnage to 19,527. (Such fluctuations in tonnages resulted from the different systems used by the British and Americans. The American system, based on an 1865 law, calculated tonnage from the hull to the first deck attached directly to it. As superstructures grew in height, the American system did not but the British system did. Thus, when an American ship entered British waters, which before 1960 was most of the world, port charges were assessed based on the British system. In return, when a British ship sailed through the Panama Canal, the Americans naturally used the British system.)

In the 1920s, a quartet of 21,000-tonners was commissioned to provide a regular service between Hamburg and New York. HAPAG therefore switched *Reliance* in 1928 to a more extensive cruise itinerary. Interior alterations in that

Reliance in white cruise livery and HAPAG's new funnel colours adopted in 1927 (Richard Morse Collection).

year resulted in an increase to 19,802 gross tons, and her final refit in 1937 brought her down to 19,618 gross tons. Her capacity was eventually reduced to 633 first class, 186 second class and 500 third class passengers on cruises. Transatlantic line voyages became a rarity, but cruises became her forte, with her world cruise being an annual event. A typical voyage was the one that departed from New York on 9 January 1936, returning 138 days later with passengers paying a minimum of $1,750 (£362) for an inside cabin without facilities to $6,600 (£1,366) for a de luxe suite.

On 7 August 1938, while preparing for a Scandinavian cruise, a fire believed to have started in a paper store caused extensive damage to the liner's interior. Hamburg-America abandoned the liner as a total loss and laid her up; in January 1940, she was sold to Krupp to be broken up.

Brabantia

(Resolute, Lombardia)

Builders 'Weser' AG. Bremen, 1920
Specifications 20,200 gross tons; 616 ft (187 m) long, 72 ft (22 m) wide
Machinery Triple expansion engines; triple screw; speed 16 knots
Passengers 335 first class, 284 second class, 469 third class, 857 steerage
Demise Destroyed in 1943.

Laid down for Hamburg-America, *William*

Brabantia *as cruise liner* Resolute, *the first large liner to sail the South Pacific* (Hapag-Lloyd AG).

O'Swald was launched on 30 March 1914. The war prevented completion, and the liner was laid up in an unfinished state until along with her sister ship *Johann Heinrich Burchard,* she was secretly sold to Royal Holland in 1916 to replace their torpedoed flagship. The Allies did not recognize the transaction and called for the ships' surrender. Adamant, Royal Holland kept the pair and renamed them *Brabantia* and *Limburgia* respectively.

Brabantia was completed in July 1920, and sailed to her new home port of Amsterdam. From there she departed on her maiden voyage to South America on 1 September. She was the largest ship ever commissioned by Royal Holland, and became its flagship as well as the largest liner on the South America run until the introduction of *Cap Polonio* in 1922.

In addition to overpaying for the twins and being short of operating capital, Royal Holland was not making a profit. The Allies were persistent in their arguments over the takeover, so to appease them and rid itself of a double burden, Royal Holland sold the pair in January 1922 to American Ship & Commerce Corporation. *Brabantia* became *Resolute,* and *Limburgia, Reliance.*

Placed under the management of United American Lines, *Resolute* was adapted for North Atlantic service. Part of her Promenade Deck was glass enclosed and her capacity was reduced to 290 first class, 320 second class and 400 third class passengers. As UAL's 19,653 ton flagship, *Resolute* departed from Hamburg on her first voyage under the American flag on 11 April 1922 heading west for Southampton, Cherbourg and New York. Her oil-fired engines, like those of her sister, gave her an average speed of 16.5 knots.

United American realized the financial rewards to be gained in off-season cruising and decided to send their two principal units to warmer climates in the winter. On 19 January 1924, *Resolute* departed from New York on a 127-day cruise circumnavigating the globe that cost a minimum of $1,650 (£382) per person. Having called at ports in the Mediterranean, the sub-continent and Asia, Captain Malman pointed the bow of *Resolute* south towards Guam and other enchanting ports in the region.

The 269 passengers were delighted to be aboard the first large passenger ship ever to cruise the South Pacific, and to accommodate them there was a wide range of public rooms. Like her sister, *Resolute's* boiler uptakes were divided so as to provide an unobstructed view down the centre of the ship. On Promenade Deck there was a succession of handsome and spacious public rooms, a smoking-room, social hall, Ladies' Parlour, Winter Garden with an arched glass ceiling, writing-room, library and a verandah. Aft was a permanent, tiled swimming-pool with a retractable glass dome, and a large gymnasium. Below on A-Deck, the dining-room extended the full width of the ship and was two decks high. For diners seeking a more intimate atmosphere there was a Grill Room aft. Cabin accommodation was on all six decks. There were four de luxe suites, twenty double cabins with private facilities and ten more with private toilet only. All cabins had an electric fan, forced air ventilation and hot and cold running

S.S."Resolute" left New York June 30th, 1934, at noon, for the FOUR CONTINENTS CRUISE

AROUND AFRICA

Calling at the following Ports - Trinidad - Bahia, Brazil - Rio de Janeiro - St. Helena - Cape Town
Durban - Lorenço Marques - Majunga Bay - Zanzibar - Tanga - Mombasa - Aden - Port Sudan
Suez, Egypt - Port Said - Haifa, Holy Land - Athens - Naples - Villefranche, Riviera - Barcelona
Tangier, Morocco - Lisbon - Vigo, Spain - Cobh, Ireland - Cherbourg - Hamburg, Germany

A postcard issued by the Romanoff Caviar Company to tell the folks at home where the cruise had reached (this was posted in Ireland in 1934) on Resolute's *Around Africa cruise (Richard Morse Collection).*

water. Other conveniences included a lift, the services of a dental surgeon and physician, a barber shop, beauty salon, electrically lit bath, laundry, valet and tailor services.

To evade Prohibition Laws, *Resolute's* registry was transferred from the American to the Panamanian flag in 1923, and with it came a reduction in port charges as the tonnage was reduced to 17,258 gross tons. *Resolute* sailed across the Atlantic in conjunction with *Reliance* on timetables that were made in cooperation with Hamburg-America Line. The latter firm were re-establishing their position and they made a deal with Edward Harriman, President of UAL, in 1926 for the purchase of three ships and an exchange of stock. *Resolute* made her last New York sailing for UAL on 26 July 1926 and her first sailing from Hamburg for HAPAG on 10 August. The change of ownership and registry increased *Resolute's* tonnage to 19,692 gross tons.

From 1928, *Resolute* was utilized almost exclusively for cruising with only a few transatlantic sailings taking place in the summer months. Her

capacity was ultimately reduced to first, tourist and third, then first and tourist and finally to 497 first class passengers. One of her last great cruises left New York on 14 January 1934, on a 137-day cruise round the world with rates starting at $1,200 (£299).

In August 1935, *Resolute* was sold to the Italian government for use as a transport. Refitted to carry 103 first class passengers and 4,420 soldiers, the 20,006-ton liner was placed under Lloyd Triestino management and renamed *Lombardia*. Voyages were made to the new Italian colony of Abyssinia (Ethiopia), to Italian Somali in East Africa and to Kenya.

Lombardia was at Naples when, on 4 August 1943, she was hit during an Allied air raid. She was completely burned out and sank. After the war in 1946, the wreck was raised and scrapped at La Spezia.

Russian Volunteer Fleet Association

Kherson
(Lena, Raetoria)

Builders R. & W. Hawthorn, Leslie & Co, Hebburn-on-Tyne, 1895
Specifications 6,438 gross tons, 471 ft (143 m) long (bp), 54 ft (16 m) wide
Machinery Triple expansion engines; twin screw; speed 15 knots
Passengers More than 1,000 in three classes
Demise Scrapped in 1924

The Russian Volunteer Fleet (RVF) was founded in 1878 at St Petersburg (Leningrad) for the purpose of forming a fleet of auxiliary cruisers to be maintained in readiness to augment the Russian Navy in times of war; the capital for this operation was subscribed on a 'volunteer' basis. The first sailing of the company was undertaken in 1880 between Odessa and Vladivostok, with a transatlantic service between Odessa and New York being inaugurated in November 1903. The service was short-lived owing to the Russo-Japanese War, and when the company re-entered the North Atlantic it was from Libau (now Liepaja, Latvia) with the *Smolensk,* commencing in July 1906.

Russian Volunteer Fleet's fifth and last vessel to ply the North Atlantic was *Kherson,* launched on 25 October 1895. She was also the smallest ocean-going three-funnel liner ever built. In 1903 she became *Lena,* a Russian auxiliary cruiser, but

The smallest of the three-stackers was Russia's Kherson *(Peabody Museum).*

was released from her duties in 1906, when her name reverted to *Kherson*, registered at Odessa.

Her first voyage departed from Libau on 23 November 1907; she made her last sailing on 25 May 1908, marking an end to RVF North Atlantic operations. In total, she made four round trips to New York via Rotterdam. The reasons why RVF suspended the service were a slump in the market, the high operating cost of ships that had limited cargo capacity, Hamburg-America's extension of operations into the Baltic and the inauguration of Russian American Line in 1906.

In 1908, *Kherson* was given a new boiler and her funnels were reduced to two. According to Noel Bonson in *North Atlantic Seaway, Kherson* then headed west and entered the Vladivostok-Vancouver service. It is doubtful whether this service was a success, and the ship was sold in 1920 to become *Raetoria*. Four years later she was scrapped.

Moskva
(Angara, Anegawa, Pechenga)

Builders John Brown & Company Ltd, Clydebank, 1898
Specifications 7,267 gross tons, 467 ft (142 m) long, 58 ft (18 m) wide
Machinery Triple expansion engines; twin screw; speed 20 knots
Passengers Data not available
Demise Scrapped in 1923

Information on this vessel is scant and difficult to locate, and was found in only one source. She was completed in 1898 as *Moskva* for the Russian Volunteer Fleet Association, and operated on

Moskva *sailed between the Russian ports of Odessa and Vladivostok* (World Ship Photo Library).

trooping voyages between Odessa and Vladivostok. During the Russo-Japanese War in 1904 she became the hospital ship *Angara,* and later that year she was sunk at Port Arthur.

Angara was salvaged in 1905 by the Japanese, and given the name *Anegawa*. Nothing is known of her service under the Japanese flag, but in 1911 she was returned to the Russians and renamed *Angara*. Again, information for this period has proved difficult to obtain.

In the First World War, *Angara* was utilized as a torpedo boat depot ship, and seized as such in 1917 by the Bolsheviks at Vladivostok. The government renamed their prize *Pechenga* and she was used by them until she was scrapped at Vladivostok in October 1923.

Smolensk

(Rion)

Builders R. & W. Hawthorn, Leslie & Co, Hebburn-on-Tyne, 1901
Specifications 7,270 gross tons; 486 ft (148 m) long (bp), 58 ft (17 m) wide
Machinery Triple expansion engines; twin screw; speed 16 knots
Passengers 50 first class, 36 second class, 1,500 third class
Demise Scrapped in 1922

Possibly the only existing picture of Smolensk *(Alex Shaw, SSHSA Collection).*

In 1906, the Russian decided to re-open North Atlantic services between Libau (Latvia) and New York. The ship selected to inaugurate this new service was *Smolensk,* launched for RVF on 7 March 1901. However, once completed, RVF employed her for transporting Russians locally. During the Russo-Japanese War, she served as the Russian auxiliary cruiser *Rion,* fulfilling the purpose of the company. Her name reverted to *Smolensk* in 1906 and, on 8 July, RVF's largest ship made her first voyage from Libau to Rotterdam and New York. Ten months later, *Moskva* (the former *Furst Bismarck*) captured the honour of flagship.

Smolensk had a beautiful external appearance. She had a clipper bow, two masts, three closely-spaced funnels, a black hull, white upper works and an unpainted wooden bridge. She was propelled by coal-burning triple expansion engines driving two screws.

On 12 November 1907, *Smolensk* made her last transatlantic sailing from Libau, having completed ten round trips. She disappeared from the western maritime press for six years, reappearing in 1913 once more named *Rion* in the Russian Navy. She was scrapped in 1922 in Italy.

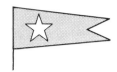

White Star Line

Justicia

Builders Harland & Wolff, Belfast, 1917
Specifications 32,234 gross tons; 776 ft (236 m) long, 86 ft (26 m) wide
Machinery Triple expansion engines; triple screw; speed 18 knots
Passengers 3,430 in three classes
Demise Torpedoed in 1918

In 1911, Holland–America Line placed an order with Harland & Wolff for a 32,000-ton steamer. The keel was laid down in 1911, and the vessel was launched on 9 July 1914 as *Statendam*. Had she sailed for HAL she would have been its largest liner, but fate decreed otherwise. She lay in an incomplete state until requisitioned by the British Government in 1917. They ordered her completion as a troop transport and gave her the name *Justicia*. The intention was to hand her over later to Cunard Line to replace *Lusitania,* hence the 'ia' ending. Instead, *Justicia* was given over to White Star Line, under whose management she entered service as a trooper on 7 April 1917.

On 19 July 1918, while on a voyage from Belfast to New York, *Justicia* was torpedoed by German submarine *UB-64* twenty nautical miles off Skerryvore, Strathclyde. Three torpedoes hit the liner, but she refused to sink. Tugs were summoned to the stricken ship and an attempt was made to tow her to Lough Swilly. In the early evening, *UB-64* surfaced again and fired another torpedo into the liner. Four hits but still floating, she was good testimony to British shipbuilding. The next morning German submarine *UB-124* sealed her fate by firing two more torpedoes into her. The unfortunate liner sank three hours later, taking with her ten souls.

Justicia *was originally laid down as Holland-America's* Statendam (Alex Shaw, SSHSA Collection).

Appendix: Notable achievements

First three-funnel liner	1881	*City of Rome*
First twin screw express steamer	1888	*City of New York*
First Atlantic crossing in under 6 days	1889	*City of Paris*
First and only steamer to go from 2 to 3 funnels	1890	*Spree*
First steamer to exceed 50,000 tons	1913	*Imperator*
First and only liner to be sunk by another liner	1914	*Cap Trafalgar*
First cinema installed on a liner	1914	*Patria*
Largest ship to sail for Hamburg-America Line	1914	*Vaterland*
Largest ship to sail for Cyprien Fabre & Compagnie	1920	*Providence*
Largest ship to sail for White Star Line	1922	*Majestic*
First gravity davits	1927	*Ile de France*
Longest bar on a liner (27 ft)	1927	*Ile de France*
First permanently fitted chapel on a liner	1927	*Ile de France*
First plane to 'take off' from a liner	1927	*Leviathan*
Largest liner built for Hamburg-South America Line	1927	*Cap Arcona*
Fastest liner placed in Pacific service	1930	*Empress of Japan*
First miniature golf course on a liner	1930	*Ile de France*
Largest and fastest ship placed on the Canadian route	1931	*Empress of Britain*
Largest ship to sail for Canadian Pacific	1931	*Empress of Britain*
First liner to be fitted with ship-to-shore radio telephone	1931	*Empress of Britain*
Largest ship to be placed on the South American service	1931	*L'Atlantique*
Only vessel to sail as a 3, 2 and 1 funnel liner	1933	*Queen of Bermuda*
First turbo-electric ship	1935	*Normandie*
First ship to have lifts for all classes	1935	*Normandie*
Largest ship to sail for French Line	1935	*Normandie*
Largest swimming-pool installed in a liner (75 ft × 18 ft)	1935	*Normandie*
First steamer to exceed 80,000 tons	1935	*Normandie*
First ship to use radar	1936	*Normandie*
First Atlantic crossing in under 4 days	1936	*Queen Mary*
Largest room installed in a liner (143 ft × 118 ft)	1936	*Queen Mary*
Largest propeller on a passenger ship (35 tons)	1936	*Queen Mary*
Largest three-funnel liner in service	1936	*Queen Mary*

Bibliography

Ardman, Harvey. *Normandie: Her Life and Times.* New York: Franklin Watts, 1985.

Bonsor, N.R.P. *North Atlantic Seaway,* Vol 1. New York: Arco Publishing Company, 1975.

Bonsor, N.R.P. *North Atlantic Seaway,* Vols 2-5. Jersey: Brookside Publications, 1978, 1979, 1980.

Bonsor, N.R.P. *South Atlantic Seaway.* Jersey: Brookside Publications, 1983.

Braynard, Frank O. *Lives of the Liners.* New York: Cornell Maritime Press, 1947.

Braynard, Frank O. & Miller, William H. *Fifty Famous Liners.* Wellingborough: Patrick Stephens, 1985

Brinnin, John Malcolm. *The Sway of the Grand Saloon.* London: Macmillan London Ltd, 1972.

Cairis, Nicholas T. *North Atlantic Passenger Liners since 1900.* London: Ian Allan, 1972.

Cary, Alan L. *Famous Liners and Their Stories.* New York: D. Appleton-Century Company, 1937.

Coleman, Terry. *The Liners.* New York: G. P. Putman's Sons, 1977.

The Cunard White Star Quadruple-Screw North Atlantic Liner, Queen Mary. Souvenir Number of the Shipbuilder and Marine Engine-builder. London: The Shipbuilder Press, June, 1936: reprint edition Cambridge: Patrick Stephens Ltd, 1972.

Foucart, Bruno; Offrey, Charles; Robichon, François; & Villers, Claude. *Normandie: Queen of the Seas.* New York: Vendome Press, 1985.

The French Line Quadruple-Screw Turbo-Electric Liner Normandie. Souvenir Number of the Shipbuilder and Marine Engine-Builder. London: The Shipbuilder Press, June, 1935; reprint edition Cambridge: Patrick Stephens Ltd, 1971.

Gordon, Malcom R. *From Chusan to Sea Princess.* Sydney: George Allen & Unwin, 1985.

Greenway, Ambrose. *A Century of North Sea Passenger Steamers.* London: Ian Allan, 1986.

Kludas, Arnold. *Great Passenger Ships of the World,* Vols 1-5. Cambridge: Patrick Stephens Ltd, 1975-1977.

Maber, John M. *North Star to Southern Cross.* Prescot: R. Stephenson & Sons Ltd, 1967.

Maddocks, Melvin. *The Great Liners.* Alexandria: Time-Life Books, 1978.

Maguglin, Robert O. *The Queen Mary.* San Diego: Oak Tree Publications, 1985.

Maxtone-Graham, John. *The Only Way to Cross.* New York: The Macmillan Company, 1972.

McCart, Neil. *20th Century Passenger Ships of the P & O.* Wellingborough: Patrick Stephens, 1985.

McLellan, R. S. *Anchor Line 1856-1956.* Glasgow: Anchor Line Ltd, 1956.

Miller, William H. & Hutchings, David F. *Transatlantic Liners at War.* New York: Arco Publishing Inc, 1985.

Mills, John M. *Canadian Coastal & Inland Steam Vessels 1809-1930.* Providence: Steamship Historical Society of America, 1979..

Musk, George, *A Short History and Fleet List of the Canadian Pacific.* London: Canadian Pacific Railway, 1961.

Musk, George. *Canadian Pacific*. London: David & Charles, 1981.

Newell, Gordon & Williamson, Joe. *Pacific Coastal Liners*. New York: Bonanza Books, 1959.

Ransome-Wallis, P. *North Atlantic Panorama 1900-1976*. London: Ian Allan Ltd, 1977.

Simpson, Colin. *The Ship That Hunted Itself*. New York: Stein and Day, 1977.

Smith, Eugene W. *Passenger Ships of the World Past and Present*. Boston: George H. Dean Company, 1963.

Talbot-Booth, Paymr Lieut-Comdr E. C. (ed) *Ships and the Sea*. London: Sampson Low, Marston & Co Ltd, 1938.

Wall, Robert. *Ocean Liners*. New York: E. P. Dutton, 1977.

Wilson. E. A. *Soviet Passenger Ships 1917-1977*. Kendal: World Ship Society, 1978.

Periodicals

Lloyds Registry of Shipping

Marine News (Journal of the World Ship Society, England)

New York Times

Steamboat Bill (Journal of the Steamship Historical Society of America)

Index

Docked in New York in September 1939 were Ile de France *(closest to camera)*, Normandie, Queen Mary, Aquitania *and* Rex *(Peter M. Warner Collection).*